KIN⬚
SYS⬚⬚

ALSO BY DR FRANK J. KINSLOW

The Secret of Instant Healing

The Secret of Quantum Living

The Secret of Everyday Bliss

*Beyond Happiness: Finding and Fulfilling
Your Deepest Desire*
(available November 2013)

All of the above are available at your local bookstore,
or may be ordered by visiting:

Hay House UK: **www.hayhouse.co.uk**
Hay House USA: **www.hayhouse.com**®
Hay House Australia: **www.hayhouse.com.au**
Hay House South Africa: **www.hayhouse.co.za**
Hay House India: **www.hayhouse.co.in**

THE
KINSLOW SYSTEM

Your Path to Proven Success in Health, Love and Life

Dr FRANK J. KINSLOW
THE ORIGINATOR OF QUANTUM ENTRAINMENT®

HAY HOUSE

Carlsbad, California • New York City • London • Sydney
Johannesburg • Vancouver • Hong Kong • New Delhi

First published and distributed in the United Kingdom by:
Hay House UK Ltd, Astley House, 33 Notting Hill Gate, London W11 3JQ
Tel: +44 (0)20 3675 2450; Fax: +44 (0)20 3675 2451
www.hayhouse.co.uk

Published and distributed in the United States of America by:
Hay House Inc., PO Box 5100, Carlsbad, CA 92018-5100
Tel: (1) 760 431 7695 or (800) 654 5126
Fax: (1) 760 431 6948 or (800) 650 5115
www.hayhouse.com

Published and distributed in Australia by:
Hay House Australia Ltd, 18/36 Ralph St, Alexandria NSW 2015
Tel: (61) 2 9669 4299; Fax: (61) 2 9669 4144
www.hayhouse.com.au

Published and distributed in the Republic of South Africa by:
Hay House SA (Pty) Ltd, PO Box 990, Witkoppen 2068
Tel/Fax: (27) 11 467 8904
www.hayhouse.co.za

Published and distributed in India by:
Hay House Publishers India, Muskaan Complex, Plot No.3, B-2,
Vasant Kunj, New Delhi 110 070
Tel: (91) 11 4176 1620; Fax: (91) 11 4176 1630
www.hayhouse.co.in

Distributed in Canada by:
Raincoast, 9050 Shaughnessy St, Vancouver BC V6P 6E5
Tel: (1) 604 323 7100; Fax: (1) 604 323 2600

A catalogue record for this book is available from the British Library.

ISBN: 978-1-78180-142-0

Printed and bound in Great Britain by TJ International, Padstow, Cornwall.

To my readers, with great appreciation.

CONTENTS

PART III: QE Applications for Everyday Living

INTRODUCTION

Hello and thank you for taking time to pick up this book. I have no doubt that what you hold in your hands has the potential to profoundly influence your life on many levels and in so many ways. I would like to take just a moment to introduce myself. I am the discoverer and developer of Quantum Entrainment® (QE™), a groundbreaking technique that has become a common but vital part of the lives of healing professionals and laypeople the world over. You will find QE to be more like a friend than a technique. It comes not from the outside but from within, beyond the furthest reaches of mind where peace and harmony abide. QE is a return to our most primal essence where the first spark of individuality was ignited at the dawn of consciousness. It is a realization, mystical and mundane, subtle and overwhelming, in its compassion for the human condition. It is yours, and it is but a heartbeat away.

I did not set out to create a universal healing technique. (I've included more details about my discovery of QE in "The Story of Nothing, and How It Is Changing the World," which can be found toward the end of the book.) But because of my unique history and a dogged desire to simplify and throw out what was not useful, the process known as Quantum Entrainment floated up, ever expanding into my consciousness like a bubble rising from the bottom of a quiet pond. *Pop!* And that was that. Quantum Entrainment was born. It came fully formed and ready to take on this world of chaos, conflict, and pain. Soon after followed the Universal Principles of Lucid Living to inspire and guide us beyond our limited lives and beyond the collective suffering that we have come to accept as normal. Quantum Entrainment, its applications in daily life, and the Universal Principles form the three pillars of The Kinslow System™.

The Kinslow System offers the basic tools and instruction booklet to not only lift us above the calamity and conflict of life, but to also show us how to pass on our newfound joy to others. Humanity is not done evolving. In our quiet moments, when we see the suffering that flickers and flares in the souls of this world, we know there is more to us. Quantum Entrainment and The Kinslow System stand at the promontory between darkness and beauty, waiting for our eager embrace. First we must retire within to appreciate our own inner divinity; then we only have to reach out and touch the light. It is just that simple.

No matter how deeply we delve into life or on which of the infinite levels we choose to examine it, we will always find The Principle of Dynamic Stillness at work. The Principle of Dynamic Stillness explains that motion comes out of stillness, energy erupts from nothing, and order is inherent in disorder. All life is a reflection of these two seemingly opposite qualities of stillness and activity. A study of life, your life and my life, is incomplete if it does not take into account the two forces of The Principle of Dynamic Stillness.

The Kinslow System is structured in just that way. It is a complete system that effortlessly applies this law toward the realization of your complete and full potential. Making use of proven techniques and applications within The Kinslow System will literally affect every aspect of your life. It is so normal and effortless you will often find improvements in areas of your life you didn't even know needed improving. It is quite remarkable, and it is completely natural.

The Kinslow System is guided by the QE Principles for Lucid Living. The QE Principles are signposts along the path to living fully and free from suffering. They are universally applicable. Each principle integrates the circumstances of your everyday surroundings with that part of you that is your essence, beyond time and space. Your inner and unbounded essence then becomes the unshakable foundation upon which you will build a dynamic, fulfilling, and abundant existence. You will find that you can always fall back on the QE Principles no matter how chaotic or uncomfortable life may become.

In addition to the QE Principles, The Kinslow System has two main arms of knowledge: the inner teachings for exploring the mystery and magic of your essence, the silent side of life; and the outer, action-oriented arm of knowledge. The silent side of The Kinslow System embraces all of the Quantum Entrainment techniques, including The Gate and Pure Awareness techniques, The Quantum Entrainment Triangulation Technique, Refined QE, QE Intention, and the concepts of Eufeeling ("euphoric feeling") and QE Awareness. The active side of The Kinslow System comprises all of the applications for these techniques, including Remote and Emotional QE, Group/World Peace QE, Kid's QE, and QE for relationships and financial concerns, loving, working, sleeping, and even brushing your teeth. In this book you will find these QE applications and many more. When you are practicing The Kinslow System, you are living in open harmony and are well on your way to becoming fully human.

Even though the QE techniques and experiences alone are of enormous value, I didn't want this book to be just an echo of previous works. So I have added five completely new chapters and more than 24 new QE applications for you to rejuvenate and regenerate your life. The new QE applications will open vibrant vistas that I am sure will excite and inspire you. You will have access to scores of awareness experiences all designed to improve your proficiency and refine your appreciation of pure awareness, Eufeeling, and ultimately this most precious gift we call life. Why do all that? Of course, to ignite the passion of becoming fully human.

This book answers the questions "Who am I, and what is my purpose?" by offering you direct access to, and healing of all levels of, your existence from the nothingness of pure awareness to its abundant and infinite forms that shape the world you live in. Its reading will open to you what it means to become fully human and then how to live that fullness. As it turns out, 99 percent of us humans are only living half our life, but filling our full potential is not as hard as you might think. In fact, it is not hard at all. It turns out that living life in fullness is really quite simple.

In Chapter 1, you will be introduced to five of the QE Principles for Becoming Fully Human, showing you how simple it will be for you to invite harmony, growth, and prosperity into your life. Chapter 1 identifies the major problems in basic concerns that we face in this chaotic and all-too-often unfriendly world. In the chapters that follow, you will learn how to practically eliminate those problems with the minimum of fuss and a maximum of fun. This book is a practical guide to improving . . . well, *everything*. Use it to remove from and add to, fiddle with and fine-tune, and ultimately build your life on the unerring principles of change, growth, and prosperity.

In this book I have drawn the techniques and experience exercises from four of my earlier works, *The Secret of Instant Healing, The Secret of Quantum Living, The Secret of*

Everyday Bliss, and *Beyond Happiness.* The emphasis of this book is on experience, and therefore, I have kept any discussion of philosophy to a bare minimum.

This book is divided into three sections. In Part I most of the material was taken from *The Secret of Instant Healing* and *The Secret of Quantum Living.* If you are familiar with those books, then the review should be helpful, but be careful, as there is new material scattered throughout that section. The chapter "The One-Minute Meditation" is an example. I suggest you reread all of the techniques and the new material where you find it. If you are a first-time reader and tend to read a book by skipping pages and chapters, you can do that, but first I strongly recommend that you read and practice the techniques in Part I, completely following each chapter in order. Then read at least "How to Have a QE Intention" and "QE Intention for Emotional Distress" from Part II. After that, feel free to enjoy the chapters in any order that draws your interest.

⊙

Part I will introduce you to the QE Triangulation and Refined QE techniques. These two procedures are the backbone of the QE experience. Additionally, you will enjoy the simple experience exercises that support those techniques.

Part II will initiate three of the most compelling entities in the quest for fulfillment and freedom from suffering: Eufeeling, QE Awareness, and the genuinely profound QE Intention. In the last chapter of Part II, "Crafting the Perfect Relationship," you will embark upon what I am sure will be an exhilarating personal exploration into the mystery and mastery of interpersonal relationships. In this chapter you will discover with ease and effectiveness the three-step process for creating spontaneous and loving relationships.

Part III invites you to practice and play with more than 30 QE experiences, most of them appearing in print for the first time. Some of the topics you will be exposed to are QE for hunger and overeating, computer QE, smelling your Eufeeling, problems with people, traveling with QE, helping children manage stress, sleeping and insomnia, mood monitoring, and more.

I am especially excited to introduce you to the chapter "Hosting a QE Practice Group." Here, you have a step-by-step guide that explains how you can host your own Quantum Entrainment Practice Group. There is no quicker or more satisfying way to enjoy the delight of becoming fully human than by sharing QE with others. In a QE group, your results are magnified and reflected back to you exponentially. QE Practice Groups improve your QE healing and harmony skills while building fulfilling, meaningful friendships with other group members. In essence, you have everything you need to host your own QE Practice Group contained between the covers of this very book.

For you, I saved the best for last. The final chapter, "The QE 90-Day Program," outlines the ideal program for you to reach QE momentum and spontaneously enjoy the bliss of inner quiet along with dynamic and successful outer activity. Think of how old you are and then multiply by four. That is the number of 90-day periods you have lived. Just think, by following the suggestions in this single chapter, you can completely renew your life in just one more 90-day period. QE is effortless, and the amazing thing is that The QE 90-Day Program is almost effortless. In fact, that is the only way it will work . . . effortlessly. These last two chapters are the thread that binds the pearls of perfection scattered throughout this book.

I've had great fun writing *The Kinslow System: Your Path to Proven Success in Health, Love, and Life;* and I'm excited that you're reading it. With it as your companion, you will release from within you the pleasure, the fun, and the exuberance for life that you were meant to have and share with us all. Approach it easily and with a sense of playfulness, and it will embrace you, whispering to you silently of the joy of becoming fully human.

Dr. Frank Kinslow
Sarasota, Florida

PART I

QUANTUM ENTRAINMENT TECHNIQUES

CHAPTER 1

Becoming Fully Human

What if I told you that you are only living half of your life? What if I said that by becoming aware of something you already have, you could enrich your abilities and talents immeasurably? Then what if I told you that you could start living 100 percent of your life today? Would you be interested? Well, I hope so because growth is a natural and effortless expression of life. It is healthy and human to explore and expand, to find meaning and purpose, and ultimately to discover what melody you are in this remarkable symphony called life.

The book you hold in your hands will show you how to do that. It will introduce you to the other side of your life, which, in most of us, is fertile but fallow. When you discover your "other side," you will find out what has been missing. From your newfound fullness, you will plant the seeds of health and prosperity and self-satisfaction.

There is nothing mystical or unrealistic in what you are about to learn. This teaching is based on scientific observation, direct experience, and common sense. It is founded on the maxim that knowledge is made of two inseparable arms each supporting the other. The two arms of knowledge are *understanding* and *experience.* Throughout the rest of this chapter, I will introduce you to powerful laws of nature, simple principles that when understood and assimilated will change your life forever. This is no idle boast but a reality for thousands of people, from many cultures all around the world. These principles apply directly to what is the same in all of us. They plant our feet firmly on the road to becoming fully human.

The remainder of this book is filled with dozens of proven exercises that help you find and express your deepest desires. These principles are self-evident and the exercises immediately effective. But you do not have to take my word for it. In a few minutes, you will begin proving it to yourself. The main technique of The Kinslow System is Quantum Entrainment (QE). Quantum Entrainment is a big-sounding scientific name, but don't let that scare you. QE is a simple process that is as natural as taking your next breath. If you are reading these lines, you have everything you need to begin. Through the simple QE technology, you will rapidly open your awareness to deeper meaning and appreciation. You will quickly align with your true desires and ultimate goals. With only a little attention and a little more work, the dividends will be astounding.

The Principle of Universal Harmony

Life is balance. Life is perfect just as it is. We have heard this stated many times in many different ways, but do we truly understand the depth of this declaration? Normally we consider our lives balanced if we don't overwork and instead spread our leftover time and energy between family, recreation, spiritual enrichment, and personal alone time. As it turns out, this is only part of the story. It is a relative balance of a superficial nature, which appreciably reduces our productivity, and more important, our quality of life.

Once you learn what true balance is, you will find it remarkably easy to realize it in your life every day. That is because it's natural and normal for human beings to live in balance. We all have the equipment, but we just haven't been using it in the right way. That will soon change. Following is an edited excerpt from my book *Beyond Happiness: Finding and Fulfilling Your Deepest Desire.* It will offer you an effective application of The Principle of Universal Harmony.

The Rule of Two

A simple perceptual shift in your mind can often remove much confusion in your life. Let me offer two simple rules that will help your mind make a shift that can relieve much self-imposed suffering. Throughout my adult life, I have been guided by these two simple axioms of insight. These two rules have afforded me both comfort and direction. The first one is The Principle of Universal Harmony: "Life is harmony." That is, there is always order in the universe, even when there appears to be none. The second dictum is this: "The world is not as I see it." It is impossible for me to know, feel, or perceive everything for any given situation; and therefore, my comprehension has to be incomplete. For me, these simple aphorisms have had a profound influence on my personal evolution. If the world were not harmonious, then I might accept suffering or limitation as being natural. If I felt that my view of the world was complete, then I might feel that my position was the "correct" one. Whenever I became stuck or in a rut, I reminded myself that life is basically joyful and that my perception was not reflecting that reality.

I soon began to see behind the scenes. Slowly these two simple rules persuaded me to loosen my grip and let life pass by like a meandering melody. Actually that makes for a good analogy. Music is enjoyed to its fullest when we let the melody flow through our consciousness like a river. If we try to hold on to even a single note, we miss the synergy of the composition. Our lives, like music, should be free to flow. Holding on to people, ideas, and things disrupts the flow and ruins the melody.

You and I are the same, and we are completely different. We bond through our sameness. Our differences add sweetness to our sameness. When these two opposites find balance, all things benefit. This has always been the formula for complete and prosperous living. I am writing to tell you this, not because I think that you don't know it, but because you may have forgotten it. I live by these two principles, not because of some cumbersome philosophy, but because they come to me from my previous life as a child. They are the beacons of childhood before time was taught and space filled with the "necessary and practical" tools for successful living. If you should wish to explore the validity of these two simple rules for yourself, don't start by remembering what was forgotten. Start where you are right now, before memory or hope can take hold.

The Principle of Dynamic Stillness

The Principle of Dynamic Stillness reveals that motion comes out of stillness, energy erupts from nothing, and order is inherent in disorder. This principle is not often realized because we tend to place value on getting things done, and we fail to realize that all created things—cosmic gas, single-celled amoebas, and ballpoint pens—issue forth from absolute stillness. That's right: every thing and thought in creation is born of stillness. Quantum physics has identified this stillness, this unmoving non-energy as implicate order. It is the non-form from which all form, and the energetic interaction between the infinity of forms, issues forth from the fires of creation. It is the gap between each and every thought in each and every one of us, generation after generation.

Understanding this extraordinary principle is not enough. Only after we have come into direct contact with this unbounded non-energy can we tap into the harmony and power of creation. As you will soon experience for yourself, the ability to contact absolute stillness is inherent in humanity, and it takes only a shift in perspective to realize it. Contact is made not with our bodies or our minds, but with uncomplicated awareness. It is out of innocent awareness of absolute stillness that we are transformed around that transcendent template of harmony, health, and love.

The Principle of Rest and Resurgence

The Principle of Rest and Resurgence informs us that when we become aware of stillness, life reorganizes in our favor. As we have been discussing, there are two sides to life: the active side and the quiet side. When we have awareness of the silent side, abundance is increased in the active side. Traditionally, we endorse the active and ignore the silent side. We may think that a good night's sleep and a few quiet moments leafing through the newspaper over a cup of coffee will fill our daily quota for rest. Not even close.

Chances are you live in an industrial society fascinated with and focused on *doing*. Think about it. How often during your day do you actually do nothing? If you find yourself with a few extra minutes on your hands, in all likelihood that free time has been imposed upon you. You might find yourself waiting for someone who is late for a meeting or with a few unexpected minutes somewhere during your day. What happens? You look for something to do, right? You might pick up a book or a magazine and begin reading, check your voice mail, or tap out a text message about how bored you are just sitting around waiting for something to happen. When you apply The Kinslow System, you can never be bored.

Somehow it has become ingrained in our psyche that we must keep moving. We feel that if we are not doing something, then we are wasting time. We may even feel guilty for taking time for ourselves.

"It's only natural," you may point out defensively. "How else are we going to evolve into more effective human beings? And after all, nature abhors a vacuum." While this is true for nature, it is not your true nature.

"Well, didn't you just say that we're born to grow?"

Yes, I did say that we are born to grow. But if we want to know what it is like to be fully human, we must start by doing something of great impact, something that we know is absolutely true but has heretofore been grievously ignored. We must rest.

Many people think that more activity brings more success. They feel that long hours of hard work is the best way to get them what they want. Unless what they want is a stressed life bursting of broken relationships and mounting health problems, then they are wrong. Success, in its deepest sense, is based on rest. What does that mean? Simply this: a rested body and mind will become more productive than a body and mind that is not rested. But what do I mean by rest? I'm glad you asked.

We humans are commonly aware of three major levels of rest. Those levels are waking, dreaming, and deep sleep. When we are awake, our minds and bodies are more active than when we are deeply asleep. When we are dreaming, our minds and bodies are not as active as when we are awake and not as rested as when we are in deep sleep. In the March 27, 1970, issue of *Science* magazine, Dr. Robert Keith Wallace published a paper that established a fourth major state of rest, which was deeper then even deep sleep. Dr. Wallace called it a "wakeful hypometabolic physiologic state," but for our purposes here we can just say that it is a "really, really deep level of rest." The interesting thing to note about this deepest level of rest is that, unlike deep sleep, your mind is actually very alert while you are experiencing it.

In later work, Dr. Wallace went on to show that this state of really, really deep rest was really, really beneficial for our bodies, minds, and our ability to live a productive, fulfilling life. And so it has been proven that when we become aware of this state of deepest rest, the other three major states of rest are brought into a condition of balance. In other words, it is not a luxury but a necessity that we experience this fourth state of deepest rest. And as you already know, balance is necessary for becoming fully human.

Now you might ask, *What can I do to experience this state of deepest rest? Do I have to sit in a pretzel-like posture, run ten miles a day, or practice positive thinking?* No, no, and no. When you go from one state of rest to another, it is a natural function of your body-mind, isn't that right? When you are tired and want to fall asleep, all you have to do is stop moving and you will naturally fall asleep. You also naturally slip between deep sleep and dreaming states routinely and without effort. When you have had enough rest, you wake up naturally. This state of deepest rest is also natural and therefore experienced effortlessly.

Effortlessly means you do not have to try. Did you ever try to fall asleep? When you did, the effort of trying to fall asleep actually kept you awake . . . didn't it? The same is true when you experience this deepest level of rest. If you try, it will not happen.

"Well," you ask, "how can I do something without trying?"

That's where Quantum Entrainment comes in. QE shows you how to naturally shift from your waking state into your deepest state of rest. As I said before, this is a natural occurrence for human beings but one we have been ignoring for a long time. It was really up to our parents and our teachers to show us how to do this, but they were unaware of it because their parents and teachers were also unaware of it. I'll develop this idea later in the book, but for now let's just focus on finding and experiencing this deepest state of rest within ourselves.

Before you naturally fall asleep, you become aware that you are tired. When you awaken from sleep, you again become aware that the sleep period is over and it is time to start your day. Here we are not so interested in whether you are falling asleep or waking up, but we are more interested in what you are aware of as you transition from waking to sleep and sleep to waking. So let's take a minute to talk about your awareness.

The most distinguishing aspect of being awake is being aware. During deep sleep and most of the time while dreaming, you are unaware. If you are like most people during your waking hours, your awareness just seems to wander through your mind lost in thought. You run on a kind of autopilot until you need to focus more clearly. It's like driving your car. Most of the time that you're driving, your mind is elsewhere. Then when you see the red brake lights of the car in front of you, you immediately become aware of the here-and-now.

Your awareness is also your starting point to enter into the condition of deepest rest. You actually pass through this level of deepest rest every time you change from one state of rest to another. When you go from waking to sleeping or sleeping to dreaming, you always slip into the deepest level of rest between them. It's like having three pools. One pool would be a swimming pool, the second would be a hot tub, and the third a sensory-deprivation flotation tank.

The swimming pool represents your waking level of activity. The hot tub, which helps you release the physical and emotional tensions of the day, would be like your dreaming state. The sensory-deprivation tank, of course, would be like deep sleep. If you want to go from one pool to another, you must first climb out of the one you are in before you can enter the second one. For instance, if you want to go from the swimming pool to the hot tub, you must first climb out of the swimming pool and then into the hot tub. Likewise, if you want to go from the hot tub to the sensory-deprivation tank, you must climb out of the first in order to enter the second. Pretty simple, yes? When you are between pools, you still exist but you aren't receiving the benefits from any of the three pools. You are in a kind of limbo as you move from one pool to the other. This analogy will help you understand where the deepest level of rest can be found and ultimately how you can experience it.

Sometimes you will notice that just before you fall asleep, your mind becomes free of worldly thoughts and feelings. You are momentarily in a kind of limbo where your mind is awake, but you're not really thinking about anything in particular. This is a momentary awareness that is as gentle as it is fleeting. It is a quiet, peaceful state that softly dissolves into the unconsciousness of deep sleep. When you wake up naturally, you may also notice this same quiet, peaceful state of awareness just before your mind starts ticking off thoughts about the things you must do in the coming day. In our analogy of the three pools, this gentle state of awareness without thoughts is like the time you are moving from one pool to another. Every time we move from one state of rest to another, we pass through this peaceful state of pure awareness. And that is a good name for it: *pure awareness.* From here on, I will refer to the state of deepest rest as pure awareness.

So now you know about the four major states of awareness that you experience: waking, sleeping, dreaming, and pure awareness. In the next chapter, you will begin learning how you can become aware of pure awareness and "use it" to balance your life on your way to becoming fully human. But, hold your horses, because before you do, we still have a few more guiding principles to talk about. And I think it would be a good idea if we started by looking at how much deep rest from pure awareness it will take to balance and sustain a very active lifestyle.

The Principle of Progress

Once The Principle of Rest and Resurgence becomes a part of your life, The Principle of Progress automatically springs into action. The Principle of Progress reveals that the more stillness you invite into your life, the more organized and dynamic your activity will become.

Its impact is felt in two distinct ways. When awareness of pure awareness balances the waking, deep sleep, and dreaming levels of living, your activity will become more orderly and dynamic. More order and more energy means that your level of success rises appreciably, and that success is obtained more easily and quickly. Let's take a moment to see how The Principle of Progress actually works.

If we sleep only a little during the night, then what we do during the day is less efficient and less enjoyable. If we get a full, revitalizing night's sleep, the opposite is true. Tasks that take effort when we are tired are accomplished with ease and accuracy after a good night's sleep. We tend to be less negative when we are rested. Time passes more quickly, and we might even find ourselves stepping lively while humming a happy little tune. This is an example of a deeper rest resulting in more energetic and fulfilling activity. It is true that the deeper our rest, the more energetic our activity. Until now deep sleep was the deepest rest we knew. And even though pure awareness, the very deepest level of rest that Dr. Wallace researched, is as natural as the other three, we seem to have forgotten about it. That's where Quantum Entrainment comes in.

When you do QE, you "remember" pure awareness. You become consciously aware of pure awareness while you are awake. While this is slightly inaccurate, I can permit it for now as it will help further your understanding. I will adjust this thinking once you've had the actual experience of pure awareness and are ready to increase your energy and improve your productivity as a result.

So here's the point. It is true that we experience pure awareness every time we go from one state of rest to another. But if we are not aware of it when it happens, it is useless to us as a tool for greater prosperity, productivity, and fun. It's like a thirsty man who dips his cup into a cool well of water upside down. When he removes the cup, it is empty. So to fill our "becoming fully human" cup, we must be aware of pure awareness, and that is what Quantum Entrainment teaches us to do. We do Quantum Entrainment during our waking state and immediately become aware of pure awareness. Doing QE shows us how to experience our deepest level of rest while we think and act and live. Now do you see what we have done? We have completed our life. We have added the absolute silence of pure awareness to support the dynamic side of life. We are no longer lop-sided, an inverted pyramid of fervent activity that is easily toppled. The base of our pyramid is planted firmly in pure awareness, and from that foundation of deepest rest, we create and live and love completely.

Naturally your next question is how much work it takes to do Quantum Entrainment and experience the deepest level of rest while awake. The answer is almost none. Remember that awareness of pure awareness is natural. That means that you already have everything it takes to do it. Just because you have not done this in the past does not mean that it is not natural for you to do now. It is actually harder not to be aware of pure awareness than it is to be aware of it. You can look at it like this: How hard is it for you to fall asleep when you're tired? Effortless, right? All you need to do is stop moving and lie down long enough to

let sleep overtake you. You simply create the proper conditions for sleep, and from there the whole process is automatic. It is exactly the same when you become aware of
pure awareness.

When you do Quantum Entrainment, you create the
best environment for experiencing pure awareness. QE is
like offering a sleepy person a bed. Once he lies down, falling asleep is effortless. Once you begin QE, experiencing
pure awareness is effortless. So now that you have become
aware of pure awareness, what do you do? The answer is
. . . nothing. That's right! Once you become aware of pure
awareness, you don't have to do anything else. Like the
effortless rejuvenation your body and mind get from deep
sleep and dreaming, so awareness of pure awareness will
rejuvenate and energize, and organize your life naturally,
completely, and effortlessly. Some say this is amazing.
What I think is amazing is that we have ignored the silent
side of our life in favor of ever-increasing activity and the
suffering it breeds.

Let's continue. Now I'm pushing this analogy to its
limits, but bear with me just a little further so I can make
this point. Let's say that you were never taught how to fall
asleep. Whenever you became tired, you were encouraged
to keep working, to keep active, so that you could get more
work done. The idea was that if you took time to sleep,
then that was wasted time—time you could have been
achieving something "practical" in the world. You would
do what you were taught and continue to force yourself
to be active, denying your body and mind the restorative
powers that sleep offers. Now let's say that you become so
sleep deprived and imbalanced that every aspect of your life
reflects joyless effort. You begin to develop digestive issues,
you gain weight, and eventually you have heart problems

or diabetes. Your mental faculties are dull, weak, and scattered; and you live in a state of constant irritability teetering on anger, or you become depressed. You escape for hours becoming addicted to television, overeating, alcohol, or drugs, or, oddly enough, more activity. You are unable to sit still for very long and enjoy the quiet pleasures of life. Relationships become too hard to maintain because you just don't have enough energy or time to invest in them. You feel that you must always be doing something because when you're not, a great weariness overtakes you. Does this sound familiar? Of course, I have just painted a picture of modern, industrialized man overwhelmed by the speed and diversity it takes just to get out of bed in the morning.

Of course you know that all of these maladies and distortions are aberrations. And you also know that a single good night's sleep would go a long way toward naturally healing them. Taking time for a full night's sleep on a regular basis would touch every corner of your world with a sparkling energy and a renewed zest for life.

All you did to arouse your healing was balance the waking state of activity with the relative rest states of dreaming and deep sleep. The Principle of Growing Success is invoked, and harmony is reestablished without any effort on your part. You don't have to work on your relationships because what they were lacking was the increased loving energy that comes from balanced living. Your body and mind will quickly respond to the healing influence of regular sleep. Your irritability and depression evaporate, and you are on the path to healing everything that is you: your relationships, job, family, body, mind, and soul.

You see, you didn't have to work much on the individual symptoms of your life when the problem was lack of sleep. You simply added sleep to balance over-activity, and the symptoms disappear on their own. It is exactly the same when you begin becoming aware of pure awareness. Remember that without pure awareness, waking, dreaming, and sleeping are in a relative state of imbalance. They need pure awareness to complete them. Just as fatigue and over-activity were naturalized by sleep and dreaming, so the imbalance of waking, dreaming, and deep sleep is balanced by awareness of pure awareness. As soon as you consciously become aware of pure awareness, healing will automatically unfold within you, and the symptoms of your life will immediately begin to disappear.

And where do you start? You begin by doing Quantum Entrainment, of course. QE easily opens your awareness to pure awareness, naturally balancing all areas of inner and outer activity. From there, you get to sit back and watch as the petals of your world unfold to the light and joy of becoming fully human.

The Principle of Lucid Living

The Principle of Lucid Living demonstrates that when you are aware of stillness during activity, also known as QE Awareness, you are at that moment in complete harmony with yourself and all other manifestations of creation. You are fully human. When you balance the deepest rest of awareness of pure awareness with activity, you grow in fulfillment.

The ultimate progression of a human being is fulfillment. Human progress finds completion in fulfillment. Fulfillment is balance on every functional level: mental, emotional, physical, spiritual, social, and so on. If there's one thing that most of us can agree on, it is that the human race is out of balance. One of the reasons is that we measure progress in very limited and superficial terms. Common definitions of progress include continuing scientific innovation or the global spread of human rights on all levels of society, eradicating famine and disease, increasing affluence, or the elimination of war. Certainly growth in each of these areas demonstrates progress, but of a limited and narrow nature. Even if you combine the astonishing scientific and technological innovations in the last 100 years, the remarkable strides toward equal human rights around the world, and the reducing of famine and disease, it is quite rare to find an individual who is fulfilled—that is, one who has learned to balance inner peace with outer success.

Fulfillment is not beyond us but built within each of us. Fulfillment is actually our innate nature. It is not that we have to work harder or take advantage of the latest technology or make more money to feel complete. Fulfillment transcends reliance on external sources or resources. To be sure, it is enhanced and enriched by them but in no way dependent on them. Fulfillment is uniquely human, and the remainder of this book is dedicated to empowering you and your own realization of fulfillment. Before moving on, let's take a moment to explore fulfillment and how you might straightforwardly integrate it into your life.

When you rest more deeply, you not only become capable of more energetic activity but that activity is more harmonious as well. As with all the principles we have been discussing, this principle can be applied universally. All of creation expands, moves forward, if you will, on two legs: one of rest and the other of activity. Every process or thing comes under the sway of this principle. The cycle of rest and activity is the basic engine of creation and continuation of the universe. But you already have direct experience of this principle in action. Does not your heart contract and then relax? Do you not find a sudden stillness waiting for you after each inhalation and exhalation of breath? Your body is compelled to rest after a day of work. When you need to concentrate on a problem, your mind performs most efficiently when it's allowed occasional time off to enjoy lighter, more rejuvenating thoughts. Ruptured by the first rays of sunlight, the stillness of night bleeds chaos onto the day. The Earth rests in winter and grows in summer. And so this principle of rest and activity is seen in every process and every created thing.

The Principle of Progress is also active behind the observable, beyond the reach of our senses. We can see it in the wave, at the most fundamental level of creation. The wave moves up and then down. Just after it has stopped moving up, and just before it begins moving down, it is at rest. Remember how many hours of fun surrounded the simple activity of swinging in a swing? Remember as a child the thrill of accelerating upward with your eyes turned sky-ward? The wind rushing across your face forced a broad smile followed quickly by a squeal of delight. And then for one brief moment you became weightless, suspended in midair clutching even tighter at the ropes that held you tenuously to the seat of the swing. Gravity then resumed its almost constant vigil, pulling you back into your seat, and the cycle continued in reverse. This is the joy of the wave, that moment of complete rest at the end of every burst of activity.

A wave is not just the active phase or the rest phase at the end. A complete wave is both the active and rest phases together. Waves go on to build subatomic particles, atoms, and molecules, and from there the infinite array of objects and energies we can never hope to know completely.

Everything is made of waves, and therefore, every thing is dependent on rest and activity for its existence. If a tree or a rock or a person is to continue to exist and grow, it must follow this simple formula of balanced rest and activity. Failure to do so finds it succumbing to the Second Law of Thermodynamics, where it begins to degrade and eventually ceases to exist.

You might well say, "I see how this can apply to a moon rock or a piece of apple pie, but how does the Principle of Progress directly apply to me?"

Here's a good way to understand how rest and activity will directly affect your happiness, your productivity, and your sense of well-being. We regard our world and react to it through our senses. The level at which our senses function is quite gross compared to the more refined levels of creation. Molecules, atoms, and the most basic building block of creation—the waves that make them up—are beyond the reach of our senses. We know their work by what they ultimately produce: mountains, people, galaxies, and, possibly more precious than all, warm pizza.

Your senses are rooted in your mind. Mental activity is wavelike in nature and therefore more refined than your senses. When an electroencephalograph measures the activity of your brain, it is measuring brain waves, the result of, or resulting in, mental activity. Because it is wavelike in nature, it is freely familiar with that most fundamental unit of creation: the wave. Your mind is a bridge between the forms of the outer world and formless pure awareness. Most people only walk one way on that bridge, outward into the world. Quantum Entrainment is a sign on that bridge that directs you to the silent side of life, back to pure awareness. When you become aware of pure awareness, you cross the bridge into the domain of deepest rest and draw from its unbounded energy, harmony, and wisdom. Then you cross back over the bridge to expend that energy, harmony, and wisdom in the relative fields of waking, deep sleep, and dreaming.

For the sake of illustration, we could say that pure awareness is the bank in which you keep your savings account. Your "pure awareness" account taps directly into the unlimited resources of the bank so you never run out of currency. In essence, you are the bank. If you stuff your pockets full of pure awareness and then cross the bridge into the land of relative rest and activity, you will slowly, or quickly, use it up. As your pure-awareness currency, "the currency of life," diminishes, you liberate less and less prosperity and joy from life. The boost you get from the relative levels of deep sleep and dreaming alone are not enough to help you reach and maintain your full potential and personal fulfillment.

Let's say that when you returned from The Bank of Pure Awareness you placed most of your pure-awareness currency in a safe in your home. Each day you expend more pure awareness on the activities of working and loving and loafing. Each evening you return to your home to draw from the safe enough pure awareness for the next day. Soon you realize that your resources are running low, and you find yourself on an energy budget. Symptoms of your energy budget are, of course, less energy, less enthusiasm, working harder and getting less done, feeling that life is somehow offering more resistance than usual, boredom and restlessness, health issues, an increase in addictive behavior, and a feeling that you are missing something—that there is more to life than you are living. In general, when you are pinching pure-awareness pennies, the spontaneous joy and lust for life is thwarted in favor of a restricted existence in the relative world. The benefits you receive from the relative rest of deep sleep and dreaming are not enough to support your right to wholly explore and embrace peace, progress, and prosperity, the symptoms of fulfillment and being fully human.

You have two apparent pure-awareness financial plans to raise you above your limiting energy budget and allow you to draw directly from the Bank of Pure Awareness. I say "apparent" financial plans because in reality one is an illusion. The traditional teaching goes something like this: if you take time each day to make the trip to the Bank of Pure Awareness and completely replenish your supply, then you will have a new supply of pure-awareness currency to expend on each new day. The hole in this teaching is that you have holes in your pocket, and as you walk from the bank back to the rocky shores of relativity, you lose most of what you withdrew from the bank. Therefore, it is felt that you must take time out of your day and continue to make this trip to the bank and back for many years, or in some philosophical systems, for many lifetimes, before you will eventually accumulate all the currency you can spend.

This illusion has been perpetrated for countless generations, but we can set things right with this simple explanation. As you know, your mind is wavelike in nature. That means it is familiar with energy and how it creates forms. What it does not understand, cannot understand, is the formless, unbounded nature of pure awareness. Pure awareness is beyond the mind and therefore beyond the mind's comprehension. Pure awareness is not kept in a bank. It is the bank, it is the bridge, and it is every created thing beyond. It is unbounded and therefore everywhere all the time. So now it is time for us to move beyond the illusion of creating greater wealth over time to the realization that we are already wealthy right here, right now. Now is the time to open to the reality of being what we already are, and that is that we are pure awareness. Again, I will not take time here to expand on this most vital realization, as we will discuss it in greater detail later. Just know that pure awareness is the source of everything, including your mind. It surrounds and supports and penetrates all energy and form.

You are probably beginning to see the significance of this realization. That means that pure awareness, the state of deepest rest, is right here with you right now as you read this book. So you don't have to close the book and go to the Bank of Pure Awareness to make a withdrawal. You only need to become aware that you are already a multi-billionaire in pure-awareness terms, and immediately, you'll begin living in fulfillment. This is not some fluffy philosophy based on faith, belief, or hope. QE is based on sound scientific principles and is reproducible by anyone who is aware. That means you. Once you've had just a few of the experiences from the beginning of this book, becoming fully human will become an absolute reality.

What I am saying here is most profound. Please pay attention, for this insight is the single most important pronouncement around which this whole book—and indeed, your whole life—revolves. What I am saying is that you can embrace a very deep level of rest even while you're washing your car, negotiating crosstown traffic while trying to make an important meeting, or bartering for a rutabaga at the downtown farmers' market. Unlike deep sleep and dreaming, you do not have to consciously set aside a special time away from activity to become aware of pure awareness. Now you can mix the two—the deepest level of rest and the most dynamic level of activity—together. You will quickly come to realize that the things you wanted to buy with your pure-awareness currency are themselves made out of pure awareness. There is no need to buy anything, to exchange energy to get what you want. You will soon learn how to appreciate the reflection of pure awareness equally in a flower or a flat tire. Once you do, you will have satisfied the principle of progress. It is the most profound and beautiful level of human functioning, and you already have everything you need to make it happen.

When you meld these two—the pure-awareness state, the level of deepest rest, with the waking state, the level of most dynamic activity—you are actually creating a unique fifth level of awareness characterized by a feeling of inner rest or peace even while performing dynamic activity. I call this fifth level of awareness QE Awareness. In the coming chapters, I'll explain more about this most crucial and essential human condition, and then I'll show you how to immediately experience it and gently integrate it into your life.

So why wait for many lifetimes or even one lifetime to get what you already have?

"Okay, Frank," you say, "now if you would like to quit talking, I would like to get on to the business of being fully human."

I couldn't agree more. In the true tradition of gaining knowledge through understanding and experience, you have had all the initial understanding you need. Your next step will be a simple experience followed by a short description followed by a deeper experience, and then a little more description that will lead to a deeper experience still. I encourage you to read Parts I and II in order. This way you will be guided step-by-step into the most profound experiences, each building on the other. By Part III, you will have the basics of becoming fully human and so can choose the experiences that most interest you no matter in what order they may fall within that section.

I've had a great time speaking with you, and I am eager to share what is in essence a wisdom that you have carried with you your entire life. It is my honor to draw your attention to the beauty, power, and joy that you are. Discover your shimmering inner Self for yourself. Come to know the bliss that you are with absolute certainty. Never lose sight of that precious and most precocious awareness, and share it with the rest of us. Pure awareness reflects through each of us differently. It speaks to us in its own way, inviting us to show it to others. In this fractured world, shining within your Self, you will silently speak to others of the ease and the joy and the grace of becoming fully human.

Five QE Principles for Lucid Living

1. *The Principle of Universal Harmony:* Life is balance. Life is perfect just as it is.

   The Rule of Two
   - Life is harmony.
   - The world is not as I see it.

2. *The Principle of Dynamic Stillness:* Motion comes out of stillness, energy erupts from nothing, and order is inherent in disorder.

3. *The Principle of Rest and Resurgence:* When you become aware of stillness, life reorganizes in your favor.

4. *The Principle of Progress:* The more stillness you invite into your life, the more organized and dynamic your activity will become.

5. *The Principle of Lucid Living (QE Awareness):* When you are aware of stillness during activity, you are at that moment in complete harmony with yourself and all other manifestations of creation. You are fully human.

CHAPTER 2

Everyday Miracles

Place the tip of your index finger lightly in the middle of your forehead. Now pay close attention to what you feel there. What does your finger feel like against your forehead? What does your forehead feel like against your finger? Is your finger warm or cold? Does your skin feel dry or oily? Is there a pulse in your finger? Do you feel a pulse on your forehead? Quietly, but very clearly, pay attention to what is taking place where finger and forehead meet. Do this for 30 seconds.

Now how do you feel? Is your body a little more relaxed? Is your mind a little more peaceful? Certainly your mind is more centered, less scattered. Isn't this true? Before you started reading the previous paragraph, your thoughts were in motion. You may have been anticipating what you were going to learn from this book. Or you may have been thinking about the meal you just ate or are going to eat. Perhaps you were contemplating an earlier conversation with a friend or thinking about what you have to do to get ready for your trip next week. But during this simple exercise, your mind was purely present. Your awareness was simple and direct. And as a result, your body relaxed and your mind became more peaceful. Why is that? How can a slight shift in awareness make such an immediate and positive change in body and mind?

Well, I'm glad you asked. Stick with me through the pages of this simple yet profound little book, and you will learn how to wield the power of awareness to transform your life in every way. That's right. Every aspect of your health, finances, love, work, and spiritual pursuits will all be made lively and full; all you have to do is learn how to be aware. And by the way, learning this is just about the simplest thing you can do.

By learning how to be aware in just the right way, you will be able to heal physical complaints such as sprained knees, headaches, indigestion, and aching joints; quell emotional concerns, including jealousy, grief, anxiety, and fear; and take control of your finances, relationships, and sex life. It even works on your pets! The process I will teach you is simple, scientific, easily learned, and immediately effective. It doesn't require that you sit in meditation, bend your body in uneasy postures, or force your breath to conform in any way. You do not have to join a group or pay dues. It doesn't even require that you believe in it for it to work—it is beyond belief. It is Quantum Entrainment, and it is opening hearts and minds all over the world to the easily experienced harmonizing power of pure awareness.

Do I have your attention? Did I get you to put down that turkey sandwich and wipe the mayo from the corner of your mouth? Good. Attention is all you need to make QE work. *That's it.* That's just how simple it is. I will show you how to move away from the thought-strewn, multi-directional mind into the calm sea of pure awareness so that you may experience firsthand the freedom from your mental turmoil and emotional madness. As the Bhagavad Gita puts it: "Just a little pure awareness relieves a soul of great fear." The wisdom of the ancients is here at your fingertips, within the pages of this very book.

I've made some pretty strong statements, and I wouldn't do so if I couldn't back up my words with some pretty strong actions. I think I've gabbed enough for now. I would like you to experience the remarkable effects that awareness of pure awareness can have on your body. Follow the steps in the next few chapters closely, and you will be amazed by what you can already do . . . and this is just the beginning.

CHAPTER 3

How to Grow Fingers

Hold up your hand, palm facing you, and find the horizontal line, or crease, that runs along the bottom of your hand at the top of your wrist. Find the same horizontal crease on your other hand. Place your wrists together so that the two creases line up exactly with each other. Now carefully bring your palms and fingers together. Your hands should line up perfectly in prayer-like fashion.

Look at how your two middle fingers line up. They will either be even in length or one will be shorter than the other. For this exercise, you will pick the shorter finger. If your fingers are even, you get to choose either the right or the left one. It's up to you.

Separate your hands and place them on a table (if you're sitting at one) or in your lap. Examine and become aware of the middle finger you chose and think, *This finger will grow longer.* Don't move the finger; just become acutely aware of it. Do so for one full minute. You don't have to tell it to grow longer again. Once is enough. Just provide what it needs to make the transition, which is your *focused awareness.* That one finger gets your total attention for a full minute. That's all!

After the minute has passed, again measure the length of your fingers using the creases across your wrists exactly as you did before, and presto chango . . . your finger is longer! It's amazing. It's like a little miracle. However, St. Augustine taught that "miracles do not happen in contradiction to nature but only in contradiction to what is *known* in nature." So, get used to it. You will be producing little miracles every day once you "know" the secret of awareness.

During the Growing Finger Exercise, you told yourself what you wanted to happen, didn't you? You had a single thought: *This finger will grow longer.* And then it happened without any further work, mental or physical, on your part. The only ingredient you added was awareness. This is all you ever need to get things done. I know that's hard to believe, but it's true, and you'll prove it to yourself by the time you finish reading this book.

The Growing Finger Exercise is not Quantum Entrainment. QE is much, much more than what you have just experienced. The Growing Finger Exercise is just an example of what can happen when you increase your level of awareness even slightly. Awareness is the prime mover of all that you know, see, and feel; and once you become aware of that, your life will flow effortlessly like a river merging with the sea of all possibilities. Then, before long, you will look back on your life and think to yourself, *I am the miracle.*

CHAPTER 4

Stopping Your Thoughts—It's Easy!

Have you ever wondered what lies at the bottom of your mind? If you could tap into the source of your thoughts, would it improve your sex life, your health, and your ability to love and live free from worry? Where do your thoughts come from, and what possible impact could that knowledge have on your day-to-day, practical life? It turns out that uncovering the source of your thoughts has a definite and overwhelmingly positive influence on personal relations, financial success, physical and emotional fitness, and even your love life. It's simply a matter of slipping the bonds of energy/matter and experiencing what lies beyond. All things are forms of energy. For instance, the chair you might be sitting on has enough energy to effectively suspend your backside 18 inches from the floor for an indefinite period of time. Thoughts are forms of mental energy, sparks of spirit, igniting the mind and everything they touch.

Thoughts are not as solid as chairs or hairs or Kodiak bears, but they exist and therefore have form and energy. And being created things, thoughts have to come from somewhere. That somewhere is actually nowhere. Or to be more accurate, thoughts come from nothing, the nothing of pure awareness. The quantum mechanical theorist Dr. David Bohm called this "nothing" field implicate order. If you are familiar with Eastern or religious philosophies, you might know it as the void, the one without form, or simply Nothing. The source of thought, it turns out, is the same as the source of all created things, Bohm's implicate order, the "void," the vast and unbounded Nothing or what we have been calling pure awareness.

Let me ask you this: Have you ever run out of thoughts? I didn't think so. One thing we can say about thoughts is that from our first breath to our last, they are there. If thoughts are energy, and we never run out of them, then it stands to reason that the source of thought is an inexhaustible supply of energy. It also seems that we might benefit greatly if we could tap directly into our source of thought. I'm certainly not the first to point this out. Wise men and women have been trying to get us interested in this very exercise for eons. If this were possible, every aspect of our lives would be wonderfully transformed. Well, let's hold on to our hats, because it *is* possible!

We can banter about abstract theories and fanciful philosophies until we're blue in the face, but that only strengthens or weakens belief. Experience is the proof of the pudding. My job is to see that you get that experience, so let's get started.

The Stopping Thought Exercise

*Sit comfortably and close your eyes. Pay atten-
tion to your thoughts, following them wherever they
may lead. Simply watch them come and go. After
you've watched your thoughts for five to ten seconds,
ask yourself the following question and then wait, in
a very alert state, to see what happens immediately
afterward. Here is the question: Where will my next
thought come from?*

What happened? Was there a short break in your thinking while you waited for the next thought? Did you notice
a space—a kind of gap between the question and the new
thought? Okay, now reread the instructions, and perform
the exercise again. I'll wait. . . .

Did you notice a slight hesitation in your thinking—
a pause between thoughts? If you were alert immediately
after you asked the question, you will have noticed that
your mind was just waiting for something to happen. Eck-
hart Tolle, the author of *The Power of Now,* says that this
experience is like a cat watching a mouse hole. You were
awake, waiting, but there were no thoughts in the gap. You
may have heard that it takes many years of arduous practice
to clear the mind of thoughts, but you've just done it in a
matter of seconds.

Please try the exercise again. Do it for two to three minutes with your eyes closed. Every 15 seconds or so, ask the
original question or use a substitute such as: *What color will
my next thought be?* or *What will my next thought smell like?*
or *What will my next thought feel like?* The question isn't
important, but paying attention is. Watch the gap closely
when it's there; look for it when it's not. Attention will

expose the gap—the space between thoughts. *This gap is the source of thought.* It may be fleeting, but it will be there. As you regularly become aware of this mental pause, it will begin to work its magic on you.

Now close your eyes and do the exercise for two to three minutes. I'll wait. . . .

Finished? Good. How do you feel right now? Do you feel some relaxation in your body? Are your thoughts quieter? Do you feel stillness or peace?

How can this happen? All you did was observe the gap between thought; and automatically, without effort, your body became more relaxed and your mind more peaceful. That is what happens when you begin to function and live in the quieter levels of the mind. The body and mind are intimately related, and when the mind stops thinking so hard, the body gets to relax and become more rested.

Now let me ask you this: When you were observing the gap between your thoughts, were you worried about paying your bills, making dinner, or remembering your spouse's birthday? Of course not. Your mind was completely still and free of worry. It is impossible to be completely aware of Nothing and suffer from fear, anxiety, remorse, guilt, or any other discordant or destructive emotion. If you did nothing else but learn this forceful lesson, you would be able to dramatically alter your life's course toward more prosperity, creativity, and love. But there is much more.

Let's continue to discover what additional pearls of perception await us from this enlightening exercise. First, tell me what was in the gap. What did you say? A little louder, please . . . oh, you said *Nothing.* That's right, there was nothing in the gap. There was no form, sound, color, smell—nothing! Or we could say Nothing was in the gap and be equally correct. Are you beginning to see the magnitude of this simple discovery?

If you thought that you were your thoughts and emotions—your memories, hopes, and fears—then maybe you have another "think" coming. Thoughts and emotions come and go. They are relative and momentary. You, your essence, is so much more than your mind can ever dream of, and you just proved it.

When your thinking stopped, did you cease to exist? Did you go into a coma or somehow become unconscious or unaware? Of course not. You were still there, weren't you? Well, if you aren't your thoughts and you were still there, then who are you? That seems like a fair question, doesn't it? If you don't know who you are, then everything you do is baseless, without foundation. You become like a man with amnesia who is trying to live his life but doesn't really know who he is. To plant your feet firmly on the foundation of life, you must know who you are. And I can guarantee that you're not foremost a person with a past and future. You will be surprised to discover that you are, in fact, unbounded and beyond time and trouble.

Let's take a closer look to see how you are beyond time and trouble. In the gap between thought, there was Nothing. But you were still aware. You were watching when the thoughts first disappeared and were replaced by the gap. But who was watching the gap?

Now, let's see . . . nothing was there, but you were still aware. There was nothing there but awareness. Not awareness of something, but a pure awareness of Nothing. Do you have it? Do you see where we are headed? If there was nothing there but pure awareness, then you must be that pure awareness. What else could you be?

If your awareness identifies with your thoughts, memories, and future plans, you are referring to the "me." "Me" is the collected "things" of your life. "Me" is your age, your sex, your likes and loves, and your memories. But none of that exists at the moment your awareness turns inward and observes the gap between thoughts. To observe, you must be aware, right? So at that moment when your mind turned off, you were aware of the nothing we call Nothing. But you found out that Nothing is not empty. Nothing is filled with pure awareness. And now you have solved the mystery of who you are. *You are pure awareness!*

Does that sound impossible? The fact cannot be denied. Your direct perception has revealed you to be pure awareness. That's right. Before "me" was born and built into the image you recognize as yourself, there was the solitary, universal Nothing of pure awareness. Stop and ponder the profundity of this realization for a moment. Again, I'll wait. . . .

Are you awed by your own immensity? Are you getting a feel for your boundless, ever-present nature? Liberating, isn't it?

Let's think on this a little longer. Recall a time when you were a child. Now, stop to look at a moment during your adolescence, young adulthood, and the present. At each stage of your life, you had different likes, desires, and goals. Your body, mind, and emotions also changed. In fact, *nothing* stayed the same. What has remained unchanged from childhood through adulthood? It is your awareness. At each stage of your life—no, each second of your life—while your body-mind was busy becoming what it is today, you, pure awareness, stood silent vigil, a timeless witness.

Through the Stopping Thought Exercise, you were able to "go inside" as it were and watch your thinking. Then while waiting ("like a cat watching a mouse hole"), you observed the gap between thought. You recognized the gap to be pure awareness, and pure awareness to be your unbound essence—the foundation upon which the "me" part of you rests. If you, pure awareness, is truly unbounded, then you aren't limited to your mind. You, pure awareness, should be everywhere, all the time . . . shouldn't you? As it turns out, you are, and here is a simple exercise you can do to prove it to your "me."

CHAPTER 5

The One-Minute Meditation

Now that you know how to stop your thoughts, you can use this new insight to create more relaxation, rejuvenation, and fun in your life. You are ready for the One-Minute Meditation. Here's how I suggest you do it. . . .

Do the Stopping Thought Exercise you learned in Chapter 4, asking yourself a new question every 15 seconds. Ask yourself four questions so that the total meditation time is one minute. The questions you ask yourself can be any of those you learned in Chapter 4, or you can make up your own. It is not the question, but your awareness that has the power. Ask your question, and wait expectantly to see what happens. That, of course, will be nothing.

You can do the One-Minute Meditation with your eyes opened or closed. In the beginning it may be more comfortable for you to close your eyes, but you will quickly find that the benefits will be there even when you do it with your eyes open. Either way is just fine.

Do the One-Minute Meditation frequently throughout the day. Do it whenever you think about it. Many people enjoy doing it once every hour. They pick a time—say ten minutes after the hour—and when that time shows up on their clock, they take one minute for themselves. This quickly establishes regularity, and regularity leads to the most ardent results.

Some people put sticky notes on their bathroom mirror, their refrigerator, or the dashboard of their car to jog their memory. What do you write on the sticky note to remind you to stop your thinking? Nothing! Leave your sticky notes blank just like your mind without thoughts.

The One-Minute Meditation is fun and effective both in the short term as well as for lasting results. Soon you will catch yourself doing it automatically and wonder how you ever got along without it.

CHAPTER 6

The Gate Technique

I have witnessed all kinds of reactions when people discover that they are pure awareness and not the stuff and clutter their minds are filled with. Usually there is a moment of delighted surprise accompanied by a sense of freedom and lightness. That sense of euphoria can last for some time, but sooner or later, the ego wants to take back control of its mind. When it does, thoughts and things are again elevated to their exalted and exaggerated positions of importance. The frail echo of awareness fades into itself and is quickly forgotten. But this does not have to happen. Hitting all the bases in this book can ensure that you stabilize a mind-set of pure awareness.

The next step to accomplish this is to deepen and broaden the non-experience of pure awareness by increasing the amount of time that we are aware of pure awareness. To achieve this, I have developed a wonderfully simple and effective process that anyone can do. I call it the Gate Technique because it opens the gate to pure awareness as easily as if it had been oiled by the gatekeeper himself. All we need to do is walk through.

The Gate Technique creates a subtle yet profound shift in the way you see the world. This *shift* may be barely noticeable at first; however, it will deeply influence your body-mind and, from there, all other areas of your life. After just a few weeks of doing the technique, it is not uncommon to have friends comment on your relaxed features or the soft luminescence reflecting in your eyes.

It's time we got started, so roll up your sleeves and get ready to open the gate to your Self.

The Gate Technique

(Note: You can download a free MP3 version of the Gate Technique at: **www.KinslowSystem.com**. In this audio recording, I will explain to you the simple step-by-step process of the Gate Technique.)

> *Sit in a comfortable chair where you will not be disturbed for 10 to 20 minutes. Close your eyes, and let your mind wander for 10 to 20 seconds. Now go through a list of positive words in your mind. You might see the words in your mind's eye or hear them; it doesn't matter. Examples might be: silence, stillness, calmness, peace, joy, bliss, or ecstasy. You may also see or hear other words such as: light, love, compassion, space, infinity, pure energy, existence, or grace. After you have run through your positive words, go back over them again. Gently pick a word that draws your attention. Next, all you have to do is observe the word. Simply pay close attention, and wait to see what it will do.*

As you innocently watch, without interfering, your word will eventually change in some way. It may get bigger or brighter or louder. It might start pulsating, or it may get fainter and even fade away and disappear. There is no telling what it will do, but that doesn't matter. You job is to purely observe, without controlling or interfering in any way. It is like watching TV, but in your mind. How easy can this be?

As you watch your word, your mind might shift to other thoughts, or you may start hearing sounds coming from around you. For a while, you may forget that you are doing the Gate Technique. You could lose yourself in your thoughts, sometimes for minutes at a time. No biggie. If this happens, when you realize that you are not observing your word, just serenely find it again. That's it! The power of the Gate Technique is in its simplicity and innocence.

Now, one last thing, you may notice that your word occasionally disappears. That's okay. Just observe the space it left behind. You will recognize it as the gap where pure awareness abides. The gap is not a goal. It is only another of the many changes your mind will go through. Soon, all by itself, your word will return. Or it may turn into another word. That is okay, too. Just accept the new word, and watch or listen to it as you did the old one.

To review, sit quietly with your eyes closed. After a few seconds, find your word and simply observe what happens. Don't interfere—just watch. When you realize that other thoughts or noises are present, quietly find your word and begin observing again. If you lose your word, it will return or another one will take its place. Just follow along.

It doesn't matter what happens as long as you purely observe, uninvolved, what is unfolding before you. Continue the Gate Technique for 10 to 20 minutes. (Always get in at least ten minutes if you can.) When finished, do not open your eyes quickly or jump up and start doing things right away. Keep your eyes closed, and take another minute or two to stretch and slowly come back to the outside world. If you come out too quickly, you may feel some irritability or get a headache or other physical discomfort. Whether you notice it or not, your body will be very relaxed, and it needs time to transition to full activity. Your mind will want to get going, but be sure to give your body a chance to catch up—then slide easily back into your active life.

Do the Gate Technique at least once every day. However, practicing it twice a day quadruples its effects. The best time is as soon as you wake up and then sometime later. If you can't squeeze it in during the day, do it before bed. This will blissfully dissolve the stresses of the day and make for a great night's sleep.

This is important for continued success. In the beginning, reread these instructions or listen to the Gate Technique audio download every couple of days. This will erase any bad habits that may inadvertently work their way into the practice. It is common to think you are doing it correctly only to find that you have left something out or added something unnecessary. If you aren't careful to maintain innocent observation, the Gate Technique will not be as effective, and you will find yourself thinking that it's not working as well as it did in the beginning. This is a dead giveaway that some impurity has crept into your practice. After two weeks of checking your technique every couple of days, reread or replay the instructions every two weeks. This will ensure that you benefit fully from your consistent practice.

The Gate Technique teaches us to rely on nothing other than observation. What happens is quite magical. A deep healing begins without a glimmer of effort. Actually, effort of any kind is counterproductive. What the technique effectively does is bathe our psyche in the healing waters of awareness. We are actually aligning with the wisdom that made the body-mind.

When done regularly, you will experience greater energy (physically and psychologically), more relaxation, less illness, more resistance to mental and emotional stress, and improved relationships. All this is accomplished by simply paying attention. Very quickly you will notice that you are observing more and more outside of the Gate Technique during your daily activities. This technique is perfect by itself or can be added to the beginning of other practices to enhance their effectiveness. Just be sure not to change the Gate Technique itself. Remember that its power is in its simplicity; it is complete as it is. Adding to or removing anything will only make it less effective.

Soon you will be learning Quantum Entrainment, the scientific method of instant healing. While the Gate Technique is not used directly in the QE process, it does help to rarefy awareness, which is the cornerstone of QE. Done daily it will quickly establish the habit of present awareness in activity. Later, when you are proficient in healing, you can substitute QE for the Gate Technique, although many people continue to do both.

CHAPTER 7

The Pure Awareness Technique

Quantum Entrainment is so simple and yet so remarkably effective because it draws on the infinite healing orderliness of pure awareness. It stands to reason that the initiator of the QE process should know what pure awareness is and how to contact it or, more accurately, become aware of it.

The notion of pure awareness has gotten a good deal of press over the years. For the most part, those who have written about it say that it is very hard to attain and takes years of study and practice to get a handle on. I say that it is impossible to attain and you will never get a handle on it . . . *because you already have it.* You can't seek something you already possess. It's not hard—it's impossible.

This is probably why so many of us have had such difficulty realizing pure awareness. We believe it is something that can be figured out, something that can be grasped with the mind. But because pure awareness is essentially nothing, we cannot grasp it with either the hand or the mind. We can't even experience it. And this is an important point, too.

Pure awareness can only be known by the lack of experience. You know, just like when you discovered the gap between your thoughts. It was a lack of experience that you realized only after you started thinking again. Pardon my grammar, but the mind doesn't like *nothing.* It wants to play with ideas or anything else that attracts its attention. That's why it makes finding pure awareness so hard. It has to. The mind can't know *nothing,* so it has to make a philosophy to define it and a complicated technique to find it. Then it revels in conditional feelings, such as self-satisfaction and pride, in an effort to convince itself that it was successful . . . but it is actually doomed to failure.

Pure awareness can't be realized by working at it; it can be realized by not working at it. The trick is to keep the mind busy with something else and then point out that awareness was there all along. Once again, go back to how you did this when you found the gap between thoughts. You're going to do this again, but when you finish, you will be able to recognize pure awareness instantly, whenever you want to.

The process we will employ is very effective, but somewhat lengthier than the simple Stopping Thought Exercise you did in Chapter 4. You will need to find a comfortable chair and a place where you won't be interrupted for at least 20 minutes. Do not do this exercise lying down the first few times; the mind is more alert when the body is vertical.

There are several ways you can do the Pure Awareness Technique. The most effective way is to get the free MP3 audio download from **www.KinslowSystem.com**. Your second choice is to read the following experience into a recorder, and then play it back when you are ready to try it.

Another way to go through this process is to have someone else read it to you. However, there should be no communication between you and the other person once he or she begins to read aloud. At the end, silence should be maintained for two or three minutes before opening your eyes. Do not communicate with your reader until you are aware of pure awareness with your eyes open.

Finally, as a last resort, you can reread the instructions a couple of times and do the exercise from memory. This will work well but may take several attempts for you to realize pure awareness spontaneously.

If you have any questions, go to the QE website at: **www.KinslowSystem.com**. While you are visiting, drop by the QE Forum where you can interact with other "QEers" and even request a free QE session. One way or another, you will quickly come to know pure awareness. In all like-lihood, you will need no more help than what you find between the covers of this book, but if you would like more guidance, QEers are always ready and willing to help. Now let's get to the business of finding pure awareness.

The Pure Awareness Technique

Sit comfortably in your chair with your hands separated. Close your eyes and become aware of your right hand. Do not move it; just be aware of it. Pay close attention to what you feel. Can you feel your pulse or any muscle tension? Do you feel any discomfort or pain? Can you become aware of a generalized sensation, such as hot or cold, relaxation or tingling? (Do this for 30 seconds.)

Now become aware of your left hand in the same way (15 seconds). Then become aware of both hands at the same time (10 seconds). Become simultaneously aware of both wrists (2 to 3 seconds).

Spend 2 to 3 seconds for each body part from here:

- Both lower arms.

- Your elbows.

- Your upper arms.

- Your shoulders.

- Become simultaneously aware of your arms, from your fingertips to your shoulders.

- Become aware of the area across your upper back.

- Now your middle and lower back.

- Your whole back.

- Your sides, from your armpits to your hips.

- Become aware of your chest.

- Your abdominal area.

- Your pelvis; then become aware of your whole pelvic region.

- Your hips.

- Your upper legs.

- Your knees.

- Your lower legs.

- Your ankles.

- *Become aware of your heels.*
- *Your soles.*
- *The tops of your feet.*
- *Your toes.*
- *Become simultaneously aware of your big toes.*
- *Your second toes.*
- *Your third toes.*
- *Your fourth toes.*
- *Your little toes.*
- *Become aware of your legs, arms, and torso.*
- *Now become aware of your neck.*
- *Your chin.*
- *Your jaw.*
- *Your right ear.*
- *Your left ear.*
- *Your lower lip.*
- *Your upper lip.*
- *Become aware of the line between your lips.*
- *Become aware of your right nostril.*
- *Your left nostril.*
- *The tip of your nose.*
- *Your whole nose.*
- *Become aware of your right eyelid.*
- *Your left eyelid.*

- *Your right eye.*

- *Your left eye.*

- *Your right eyebrow.*

- *Your left eyebrow.*

- *Become aware of the space between your eyebrows.*

- *Your forehead.*

- *The back of your head.*

- *The top of your head.*

- *Your whole head.*

- *Become aware of your whole body. Have awareness of your whole body (10 seconds).*

- *Now become aware of an area around your body—an area about 12 inches around your body, like an oval or egg surrounding your body (10 seconds).*

- *Let your awareness expand further away from your body (5 to 6 seconds).*

From here, you should hold each object in your mind for 5 or 6 seconds:

- *Become aware of your awareness filling the whole room.*

- *Now expand beyond the room and become aware of your awareness in the whole building.*

- *Expanding beyond the building, become aware of an area around it.*

- *Expanding ever-more rapidly, become aware of the whole city.*

- *Expanding still more rapidly, become aware of the area around your city, neighboring cities, and the whole state.*

- *Become aware of neighboring states and the entire country.*

- *Become aware of all of North America and then of the whole Western hemisphere (or whichever continent and hemisphere you are in).*

- *Become aware of the entire Earth. Become aware of the planet spinning silently, powerfully, on its axis.*

- *Your awareness continuing to expand, the Earth grows smaller, the moon a silver dot.*

- *Earth grows smaller and smaller until it is just a glistening light the size of a star in the sky.*

- *Your awareness continues to expand, and the sun slips silently by. It becomes smaller and smaller until it is the size of the other stars in the sky.*

- *You become aware of the millions and billions and trillions of other stars filling the sky. All are within your awareness.*

- *Your awareness continues to expand as the stars form into the galaxy, spiraling silently, powerfully, on its axis.*

- *And still your awareness continues to expand, and the galaxy gets smaller and smaller until it is the size of a star in the sky.*

- *It is lost among the millions and billions and trillions of other galaxies in the sky.*

- *As your awareness expands, all the galaxies, all of creation, take the form of an oval or egg suspended and supported by your awareness.*

- *All of creation is contained in this single glistening cosmic egg within your awareness.*

- *As your awareness continues to expand, the egg of creation grows smaller and smaller.*

- *It is the size of a grapefruit.*

- *The size of an orange.*

- *The size of a lemon.*

- *The size of a pea.*

- *The size of a single glistening star in the sky.*

- *As your awareness expands, all of creation becomes the size of a brilliant pinhole of light suspended in your unbounded awareness.*

- *Then all of creation, that single pinhole of light, goes out (30 seconds).*

- *Now once again become aware of your whole body (15 seconds).*

- *Become aware that you are sitting in this room filled with your awareness. Everything in the room is in your awareness (15 seconds).*

- *Become aware that all of creation is in your awareness (15 seconds).*

- *Become aware of your whole body again, sitting in your awareness.*

- *Now take 2 to 3 minutes to remain seated and relaxed before you open your eyes. Maintain your expanded awareness as you begin to open your eyes. Don't be in a hurry. Take time to come out, as your awareness fills the whole room (1 minute).*

- *With your eyes still closed, slowly wiggle your fingers and toes, or stretch lightly. Be aware of your awareness permeating your body and filling the room (30 seconds).*

- *Now slowly open your eyes while you are aware that your awareness fills the whole room (10 to 15 seconds).*

- *Are you still aware of your awareness filling the whole room? Look at any object. Are you aware of your awareness between you and the object? Your awareness has always been there. You are just becoming aware of it outside of yourself. How do you feel (5 to 7 seconds)?*

- *Do you feel some sense of peace or quietness? Some lightness or bliss (5 to 7 seconds)?*

- *The quiet easiness you feel is a Eufeeling. It is a reflection in your mind of pure awareness. It doesn't matter if you feel it as joy, peace, or stillness; it is the result of being aware of pure awareness.*

- *Are you aware of your awareness filling the room right now (3 to 5 seconds)?*

- *See, it is still there. It is always there, and now you will always be aware of it whenever you want. Do it again. Become aware of your awareness in the whole room (3 to 5 seconds).*

- *Now become aware of your awareness in your whole body (3 to 5 seconds). It's there, too! Pure awareness is everywhere. It's like the coat that you forget you are wearing. All you have to do is think about it, and you will know that it is there, always keeping you warm. Whenever you think about pure awareness—that is, become aware of it—you will find it waiting for you. Wherever you are, there it is. It's like the young child of a loving mother. When the child misses her mother, she only has to look around to see that her mom is there, watching over her.*

- *Go ahead, is "Mother" watching? Become aware of your awareness filling the whole room, your body, and all of creation (5 to 7 seconds).*

That took no effort at all, did it? You didn't have to do something to find awareness, did you? You just became aware that it is there. Now you don't need a technique to find pure awareness only to lose it again when you stop the technique. You will be aware of pure awareness forever and without effort. How cool is that!

Okay, one more thing:

- *Close your eyes again and become aware of your awareness filling the room (15 seconds).*

- *Now pay attention to what you are feeling— your Eufeeling. Just identify if you are feeling peace, stillness, quiet, bliss, and so on. Find your Eufeeling, and watch it for a while (8 to 10 seconds). Nice, isn't it?*

- *Now open your eyes. Become aware of awareness all around you, and again iden- tify your Eufeeling with your eyes open. It could be the same or different; it doesn't matter. Just pay attention to what Eufeeling you are having right now (8 to 10 seconds).*

In preparation for creating a healing event with Quantum Entrainment, every now and again through- out your day, I would like you to become aware of pure awareness and the Eufeeling associated with it. For the first few times, you may need to start out in a quiet environment with your eyes closed. But after a couple of tries, you will be aware of your Eufeelings even in the middle of rush-hour traffic.

Remember to become aware of pure awareness first. Then while you are watching or feeling pure awareness, your Eufeeling will effortlessly shine through. While becoming aware of awareness is effortless, it takes the mind a little time to get used to a good feeling that is not associated with some activity. The Eufeeling is the subtlest activity in the mind, and it just takes practice to get your otherwise active mind used to hanging out on that quiet level.

Okay, that does it for now. I'm glad to have had you along for the ride. Now that you are among the newly awakened, fully savor your new awareness and the joy it will visit upon you.

CHAPTER 8

The Quantum Entrainment Triangulation Technique

Healing with Quantum Entrainment is actually realizing that you are not healing. You are not creating positive energy to overcome negative energy. You are not calling on other forces or formulas to do your bidding. You *are* creating an atmosphere in which healing will take place. QE is tuning in to the *field* (for lack of a better word) of perfect order. From there you do nothing, and everything gets done for you.

As a matter of convention, I will say "You heal" or "I healed,"but that is not strictly true. In preparation for creating a healing event, we must adopt the correct angle of entry to be successful. For me to say that we do not perform the healing is neither attitude nor philosophy. It is a simple fact based on observation. This healing presence is not a foreign force that is beyond you but your very own essence—pure awareness reflected through Eufeeling. Nothing more, nothing less.

You will be amazed by the power your awareness holds, but know that you do not own that power. You are that power and will soon experience it firsthand. You will slip beyond the boundaries that you have meticulously built these past decades in order to define the little you. These boundaries have confined your awareness to thoughts and things that have all served to strengthen your concept of *me*. However, that will be set aside the very first time you experience Quantum Entrainment.

Eufeeling

One more thing before we learn to create a healing event. I want to discuss something I introduced to you in the Pure Awareness Technique. It is something so vital to health and harmony that the whole of Quantum Entrainment revolves around it. In fact, the whole of creation revolves around it. What is it? *Eufeeling.*

A Eufeeling ("euphoric feeling") is unique in all creation. It's the first manifestation of fullness through which the stuff of the cosmos must pass before it becomes a ranch-style house, a butterfly, or a flowing river of lava. A Eufeeling is completely safe; it's the only created thing that is free of restriction and contradiction. It is completely open and free flowing.

To the mind, the Eufeeling is rich dark chocolate, a new love, and a rocket ride to heaven all rolled into one. To be cognizant of Eufeeling is the definitive goal of the mind. When it is, the mind yearns for nothing. Established in awareness of Eufeeling, the mind is safe. It can pick its way between the horrors and hardships of life and always feel that Mother is watching, waiting with open arms to protect and comfort.

What exactly is a Eufeeling? Good question. Your mind identifies Eufeelings as joy, peace, stillness, silence, unbounded love, bliss, ecstasy, and so on. Eufeelings are not to be confused with everyday garden-variety emotions, such as happiness, excitement, anger, grief, conditional love, jealousy, or fear. These emotions I call *conditional feelings* because they're borne out of circumstance—for instance, getting money, losing money, losing a loved one, getting a new job, and so forth.

I'll let you in on a little secret: Eufeeling is the Self. That's right. Your Self reflects in your mind as joy, love, and peace. Remarkable, isn't it? Your Self is beyond the sight of your mind just as the rays of sunlight that color the ocean are beyond the capacity of your eyes to see them. However, the first stirring of your Self in the mind can be recognized, and that's when you feel peace.

The point here is that Eufeelings are always pure and clear—*always.*No matter what you feel or think or do outwardly, inside you is the clear reflection of your Self, of Eufeeling.

Doing Quantum Entrainment enlivens the mind with Eufeelings, and the mind automatically becomes harmonious. From there, it reflects harmony into the environment for the benefit of all. Through QE, we spontaneously enjoy the Eufeeling flavor of the moment reflecting in our minds. We also learn to recognize this inner purity of others. We look past the reflected imperfections and see the vibrating peace and stillness of another's Eufeeling, and we recognize it as our own. It is on the level of Eufeeling awareness in which we truly are all one.

Now let's roll up our sleeves and get ready to create a healing event. We'll start with a simple case: a friend has asked you to help him with left shoulder pain and muscle tension in the upper back and neck. With QE, it is not necessary to know the cause of the condition. Healing will take place on the causal level automatically. As the initiator, you only need to know what is desired. Obviously, your partner desires relief from his shoulder pain and muscle tension. That is inferred and is also your intention. It is all the info you need.

Getting Ready to Heal

Before you start, have your partner move his shoulder (or whatever area of physical discomfort he may be experiencing) so that it creates the pain he wants to eliminate. Have him show you how his range of motion is diminished and anything else that demonstrates how the body is affected by this condition. Then ask him to grade the severity of his pain on a scale from one to ten (ten being unbearable), and note that number. It's also important to get into the habit of pretesting and posttesting. This will give you valuable feedback, especially in the beginning when you are just getting used to the QE process. If you are a physician, use the same tests you would employ for traditional treatment. For instance, a chiropractor might use orthopedic and neurological tests, palpation, and even x-rays to objectively identify the problem and determine the level of improvement.

You only need to be aware of the intention one time. Pure awareness is neither deaf nor dumb. It will know what you want better than you will. Pure awareness will know what to do and when to do it—of this you can be sure. Now you are ready to start.

Quantum Entrainment Triangulation: The Three-Step QE Process

On your partner's shoulder, upper back, or neck, it should be easy to find a muscle that is tight or painful to the touch. Place the tip of your index finger (Contact A) on a tight muscle. Push in firmly so that you can feel how hard or tense the muscle is. Then relax and let your finger rest lightly on the tight muscle. Now lightly place the index finger of your other hand (Contact B) on any other muscle. It does not have to be taut or sore to the touch. Just pick a muscle at random, and place your finger there.

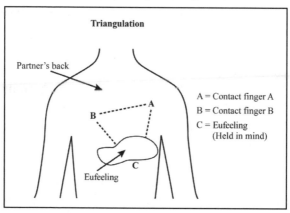

Step 1: Focus all of your attention on Contact A, and become very aware of what you feel. Take the time to

notice the heat from the muscle on the tip of your finger, the texture of your partner's skin or clothing, the tightness of the muscle pushing back against your finger, and so on. Become aware of everything you can where finger and muscle meet.

Step 2: Become acutely aware of Contact B, just as you did with Contact A. Then become clearly aware of what both fingers are feeling *at the same time.* Maintain this awareness for several seconds. While you simultaneously hold your attention on both fingers, you will also notice a separate part of you that is just watching the whole process take place. You, your awareness, is aware of both fingers. So far, you have awareness of Contact A, awareness of Contact B, and awareness that you are aware of both at the same time. It doesn't matter if you are clearly aware of this phenomenon or not; it is happening naturally, without effort.

Step 3: As you hold awareness of the two points in this expanded way, do nothing. That's right—just pay attention to what you are sensing in the tips of your two fingers and that is all. If you are simultaneously paying attention to your two contact fingers and doing nothing else, you will soon begin to feel a sense of quietness, stillness, or even peace. This is a Eufeeling generated from your expanded awareness. At this point, become aware of this sensation as you hold your awareness on Contacts A and B.

You now have three points of awareness: Contact A, Contact B, and your Eufeeling. Holding them in your awareness is called *triangulation.* Continue to be aware of all three points until you feel a change in your partner's body, particularly in his muscles. (This can take several minutes when you are first learning QE.) The change you experience might be a softening or loosening of the muscles under your fingers. It may feel as if your fingers are relaxing or dissolving into the muscles themselves. Or you may feel that your partner is generally relaxing. His shoulders might loosen, or he may sigh or take a deeper breath. If you are both standing, you might note that your partner is swaying. This is a common reaction to the very deep level of healing rest that your partner is enjoying. You may also notice that your partner is generating more body heat or even sweating.

All of these changes signify that your partner's body is healing. It is reorganizing to eliminate the disorderly pain and tension. After you observe any of these indicators, continue to triangulate by simultaneously being aware of the two contact points and your Eufeeling a little while longer. Then remove your fingers.

Congratulations! You have just completed your first Quantum Entrainment session. With just two fingers and your Eufeeling, you have eliminated your partner's suffering!

You might be wondering what your partner is experiencing while you are creating this healing event. The answer is *absolutely nothing*. Before a QE session begins, I tell my partner, "Just let your mind wander wherever it wants to go." I am often asked by partners if they should relax, meditate, or repeat their own intention. They should do *nothing.* They should not try to help in any way because if they do, it would only slow down or counteract the initiator's efforts. The reason for this is since their minds are busy with other chores, they are less open to the healing influence that QE generates. However, a mind in "neutral" will naturally and effortlessly drop into the healing waters of pure awareness.

Always make your partners comfortable. If they wish, they can close their eyes, but that is all the preparation they need. If they want to help you in some way, you can tell them that the best thing they can do is to allow their mind to wander with no direction or intent.

Quantum Entrainment works very well under the most trying circumstances. Your partner may be in a great deal of physical or emotional pain. You may find yourself performing QE in an emergency room, a crowded mall, or in any other unsettling environment; and healing will still take place. So don't think that you are limited by these things. But given the choice, a serene environment with a compliant partner is always preferable.

The QE Session in a Nutshell

- Partner describes pain (intention implied).

- Pretest.

- Become completely aware of Contact A

- Become completely aware of Contact B.

- Become aware of both A and B at the same time. Your mind feels some lightness or a sense of expansion. This is your Eufeeling.

- Become aware of Eufeeling.

- Hold awareness of all three at the same time: Contacts A, B, and Eufeeling.

- Observe partner's muscles relaxing, body swaying, breathing changes, or other signs of relaxation.

- Posttest.

CHAPTER 9

Refined Quantum Entrainment

Refined QE does pretty much what it says. It is a refinement over the QE Triangulation Technique. The QE Triangulation Technique involves three points of contact. Refined QE allows us to drop two of those points, making it all that more simple. It's like taking the training wheels off of our bicycle. Most people like to do QE Triangulation for a while until they are more familiar with pure awareness and Eufeeling. Then they feel more comfortable doing Refined QE. However, I often teach Refined QE during radio programs to listeners who have never heard of QE before. Refined QE can be done anywhere, anytime, and is as easy as shifting your awareness from one object to another. I'm anxious to teach you this surprisingly subtle and remarkably powerful technique, so what do you say? Shall we get started?

How to Do the Refined QE Technique

In preparation, find yourself a quiet place with a comfortable chair where you won't be disturbed by family, friends, pets, or phones for a full 30 minutes. You can follow the instructions below on your own, or you can ask someone to read them to you. But this person should only read what is written and not engage you in conversation. You could also record yourself reading the instructions, but be sure to leave some blank spaces whenever you're directed to remain still with your eyes closed. In addition, you can have these instructions read to you by yours truly on the two-CD set *Exercises for Quantum Living: Quantum Entrainment for Finances, Emotional, and Physical Self-Healing* available at: **www.KinslowSystem.com**. Okay, here we go:

> *Sit comfortably and close your eyes. Let your mind wander wherever it wants to go for 15 to 30 seconds. Just watch your thoughts as they come and go.*
>
> *Now become more aware of what you're thinking. The content doesn't matter; just pay close attention to any thoughts that flow across the screen of your mind. Observe with focused attention. That doesn't mean you should make a great effort to try to concentrate on them. Just be easy with a focused attention like a cat watching a mouse hole. Continue to watch your thoughts with relaxed, focused attention for one to two minutes.*

Don't read any further until you have done so. I'll wait. . . .

Have you finished attentively watching your thoughts for one to two minutes? Good, then let's continue.

As you observed your thoughts, you may have noticed that they became quieter and slowed down almost immediately . . . isn't that right? They didn't seem as loud. They became fainter and fewer in between as your thinking became softer. Remember that whatever your thoughts are doing is just right. Whether your thoughts are noisy or quiet doesn't matter; your job is to be the perfect observer. You just sit back and see what they'll do next. That's all you must do: observe with quiet attention.

Did you happen to notice that at times your thoughts stopped altogether? As your thoughts became fainter, you might have realized that they died away, and you were left alone with pure awareness. Neat, huh? But we're just getting started.

Did you also note that after you finished the first part of the exercise, you felt more relaxed in your body and more quiet in your mind?

These are the delicious benefits of becoming aware of pure awareness, whether or not you're aware of it. Soon you will be functioning on this quiet, more refined level even while you're stuck in traffic . . . but we have more to do, so let's get back to it:

> Once again, close your eyes. Innocently, and with attention, watch your thoughts as before. This time it will be easier, and you might find your thoughts quickly settling down or completely stopping. Attentively observe in this way for a couple of minutes. Then note how you feel.

Again, I'll wait. . . .

During those two or three minutes, did you feel some stillness, silence, or peace? You might have also felt joy, love, compassion, elation, or bliss. The good feeling that you experienced is your Eufeeling.

This time when you sit with your eyes closed, I would like you to do the following: watch your thoughts, and wait for your Eufeeling to rise into your awareness. Remember, your Eufeeling could be something as simple as stillness or silence, or as profound as ecstasy. One Eufeeling is no better than another. Whatever your Eufeeling is, just easily observe it. And if thoughts return, innocently observe them, too. Then your thoughts will give way to either "no-thought," pure awareness, or your Eufeeling.

Whichever is there—thoughts, Eufeeling, or pure awareness—continue to observe with simple innocence and do nothing else. This is very important: do nothing but watch your thoughts and wait for your Eufeeling. When your Eufeeling is in your awareness, focus on it clearly and intently. At times you may have neither Eufeeling nor thoughts—and this is pure awareness. Simply wait in pure awareness until your Eufeeling rises again.

Do you see how simple this is? Regardless of what appears on the screen of your mind, your position is always the same. You are the observer, nothing more. *Never interfere or try to control either your thoughts or your Eufeeling.* Believe me—everything will be taken care of for you. Did you have to work at becoming relaxed or feeling peaceful? No, it's all automatic. It's all taken care of for you through the wisdom of your Eufeeling once you become aware of it. Don't complicate it, or you will step back onto the path of struggle and suffering.

Now resume the QE process with your eyes closed just as I've previously described it. Do this session for about five minutes. When you're done, take enough time to slowly open your eyes and continue reading.

How are you feeling right now? Are you aware of your Eufeeling? Guess what? Your eyes are open, and you are aware of your Eufeeling! Isn't that remarkable? Before you had to close your eyes and dive deep within your mind to find it. But look what has happened: your Eufeeling has followed you out into activity. How cool is that?

Remember that your Eufeeling is unbounded, so it's always there. You've just been ignoring it most of your life. And you will ignore it again, but by doing QE regularly, you'll always regain it through a moment's reflection. You are building the foundation for a life that is beyond imagination. Somewhere in the not-too-distant future, you will all of a sudden realize that you are living life in bliss, beyond your greatest expectations.

Now, we aren't quite done. In fact, the best is just ahead. I'd like you to continue with the QE process as you've just learned it. Close your eyes and observe what is flowing across the screen of your mind. Watch until you become aware of your Eufeeling, and then observe it with tender attention. Not interfering, look deeply into Eufeeling. If it changes into another Eufeeling, then look deeply into the new one. Do this for three to five minutes.

When you feel the time is right, slowly open your eyes and continue doing QE. Sitting with opened eyes gazing easily in front of you, become aware of your Eufeeling. Continue to do QE. You will have thoughts, Eufeeling, and pure awareness all with your eyes opened. Continue for one or two minutes more, and then slowly stand up and look at a nearby object. While doing so, become aware of your Eufeeling. Then look at another object while still observing your Eufeeling.

When you're ready, slowly walk around the room. Feel your body moving. Feel how you balance on one leg, then the other, and the pressure of the floor against each foot. When your Eufeeling isn't there, just find it again through simple awareness. As you walk slowly around the room, engage all your senses. Pay attention to the noises in the room. Feel the air brush past your face, and run your hand over a plant or another object. Engage your sense of smell and taste. All the while, continue to return to your Eufeeling whenever you notice it's not there. Stop and become solely aware of your Eufeeling and feel how it intensifies or changes into a different Eufeeling.

In actuality, it doesn't really change in intensity or kind. You are just becoming more aware of the infinite manifestations of your Self. This is You the way you were meant to be. Not all tangled up in the ego-manipulated activities founded on fear, but just simply being with your Self. Nothing is more important or fulfilling.

You can use Refined Quantum Entrainment instead of Quantum Entrainment Triangulation if you like. They are both equally effective, but as you have just discovered, Refined QE has only one step instead of three. Refined QE gives you more freedom and more opportunities to share Quantum Entrainment with others, and that is a very good thing indeed.

Refined QE Review

- Sit comfortably with your eyes closed, and let your thoughts wander for 10 to 15 seconds.

- Watch your thoughts with simple innocence, like a cat watching a mouse hole.

- In time, your thoughts will become quieter or slower; they may disappear altogether. Continue to quietly observe whatever happens.

- Soon you will feel a good feeling—your Eufeeling.

- Observe your Eufeeling with clear but simple innocence. It will get stronger or change into another Eufeeling, or new thoughts will come.

- Whatever happens, just observe it unfolding as if you were watching a movie.

- When you open your eyes, continue this simple process of innocent observation.

- Move around the room, slowly interacting with objects.

- When you realize that your Eufeeling has slipped away, just look to see what you're feeling. Observe it for a while, and then continue to explore other objects.

CHAPTER 10

What Do I Do Now That I Can Heal?

When you finished your QE session, did you feel relaxed and peaceful? Quantum Entrainment heals the healer as well as the one requesting healing. Both you and your partner should be feeling quieter and more serene. Relaxation is the body's reaction to the healing presence of pure awareness, and peace is the reflection of pure awareness in the mind.

Remember to ensure that your partner is comfortable. The QE experience can be a little disorienting for some people. The sudden rush of pure awareness may take them away from this world for a bit. Afterward, they might need time for their mind and body to reorient to the here-and-now. If this happens, it generally only lasts a few minutes. Give your partners space until they are ready to resume.

One thing you can count on is that after the QE session, your partner will continue to heal for the next day or two. If you perform a second posttest 20 to 30 minutes after the initial session, you will almost always find that the number is getting even smaller as the problem continues to heal. Making sure that your partner transitions easily from the QE session to his or her more active lifestyle will encourage the healing process to continue unobstructed.

On occasion, especially after an extended QE session, your partners may need more time to adjust to their new body and may become tired or so relaxed that they don't want to move. If at all possible under these circumstances, make sure your partners get the needed rest. This just means that great amounts of physical and emotional stresses are being released, and a brief repose is the most expedient way for this transition to take place. After all, rest is the universal healer, and pure awareness is the deepest rest possible. If your partners can't lie down and relax right then, suggest that they go to bed early that evening. Then they will awaken to a bright new world and have an extra bounce in their step.

The best time to do your posttest is as soon as you have finished the QE session and your partner is stable. Ask your partner to once again grade his or her condition or level of discomfort on a scale from one to ten. For the example case mentioned in the previous chapter, you would have your partner put his shoulder through the same range of motion, and ask him to grade the pain and muscle tightness as he did before. This is necessary feedback for you in the early stages of learning QE, and it is also good for your partner to get a more objective view of the healing that took place in his or her body.

QE heals so quickly and easily that it often appears as if nothing has happened. The posttest, therefore, is a real eye-opener for many partners. I never get tired of watching people's faces as they perform the posttest, and a pain or restriction they've endured for 30 years is gone in 30 seconds.

QE works every time, but not always in the ways you want it to. That is because pure awareness views the big picture and knows exactly how healing should take place. There is almost always a significant relief of symptoms immediately after a QE session, and if the problem is not completely eliminated initially, then it will take just a little more time for the body to adjust. The healing will continue to take place over the next day or so and can even be felt weeks later.

It is not uncommon for me to do QE on a workshop participant in the morning and only see a minor drop on the posttest scale, but by the midday break, the pain is then completely gone. Even though the actual healing takes place instantly (via pure awareness during triangulation), a person's body may require additional time to integrate those corrections physiologically. We'll spend more time on this later.

There is no rule saying that you can't turn right around and do QE again for the same condition. If you think it will help, repeat the session. Or better yet, do multiple applications during a single session. Just keep your A contact and move your B finger to different areas. Or you can move both fingers if you wish, depending on what feels best to do in the moment.

Perform QE as many times as you like. You can do no harm. But let me caution you against thinking that more is better—that is not always the case. You should have in your mind that one short session will take care of the problem and go from there. In an upcoming chapter, I will show you how to do "Extended QE," but for now, let's keep it very simple. Deal? Good.

For all intents and purposes, you are done. But in the beginning while you are sharpening your QE skills, it doesn't hurt for you to ask your partner a few questions. Find out how he felt during the session or if any other pains are gone along with the original complaint. Inquire after his emotional well-being. Actually, ask any questions you need to know to help you more fully understand the power and potential of QE.

The whole QE process should be delightful. If you find yourself getting tangled up in the instruction, that is natural at first. The steps are seamless, but reading about them takes considerably more effort than actually doing them. Just relax into it and follow the instructions with a sense of adventure and play. Everyone can do QE. You are no different. While this technique is simple and immediately effective, it is a new skill, and you will need to practice it often in the beginning. Remember, well begun is half done. The more feedback you gather at this stage, the more quickly you will become proficient at applying Quantum Entrainment.

Practice it on everyone: your friends, family members, neighbors, and even your pets. Soon you will also learn "Remote QE," which means that you don't have to have your partner present. You can sit comfortably at home and create a healing event with your friends and family scattered all over the world.

The first several times you practice QE, I suggest that you and your partner both stand. The main reason for doing so is that you will get more precise feedback from your partner. In particular, you will notice her swaying, a sign that pure awareness is working. You will also more easily observe whether she takes a sudden deep breath, which is another indicator that QE is working its magic. It is not as easy to observe these indicators when your partner is seated or lying down.

I would also recommend that you stand a bit behind your partners in the beginning, or at least where they cannot see you. Being out of the line of sight allows them to relax rather than watch you. It doesn't matter for the sake of their healing. Quantum Entrainment will work regardless of your partner's state of mind. It is more for your comfort and concentration, as some initiators are self-conscious when they first get started and can be distracted if their partners are watching their every move.

Another practical point is that you do not have to put your fingers on the area of complaint. You can touch anywhere on the body and heal any other area, including internal organs.

I was at a book fair promoting my book *Beyond Happiness* when a fellow author approached me. He said that he'd heard I did kind of a weird thing that got rid of pain. I asked what was bothering him. We had been standing for some time, and his arthritic knee had become inflamed and swollen. I pretested him simply by asking him to stand on the knee in a way that increased the pain. Then I had him sit on a box of books. I didn't want to bend way over to place my hands on his knee, so I positioned my fingers on his shoulders. He immediately turned around and reminded me that it was his knee that was hurting. I assured him I was working on his knee.

I formed the intention and began triangulation on his upper-shoulder muscles. Less than a minute later, I asked him to stand as he did before to test the knee. He did and—I never get tired of this part—his eyes opened wide as a sense of wonder lit up his face. Pain free, he returned to his stall to sell more books than I did. My fingers contacted his shoulders, but the wisdom of Quantum Entrainment made sure it was his knee that received the healing.

Sometimes pain (or other symptoms) will worsen before it gets better. Just assure your partner that this is normal. During this time, the body needs to exacerbate the condition for a short period in order for it to heal. Continue to triangulate, and the pain will subside quickly. On rare occasions, your partner might become too uncomfortable to continue. At that point, discontinue the QE session. Perhaps you might perform QE on another problem or just sit quietly. After a few minutes, perform the posttest and see if the condition still exists. If so, do QE again. In all likelihood, the pain will dissolve with no further issues.

One last thing: since you are not doing any healing, you cannot take any credit for the results. This is a very important point. If you do not take credit for the results, you cannot be *attached* to the results. Do you see where I'm going with this? If you are not attached to the results of your QE session, then you are able to accept whatever results appear. Complete acceptance of the fruits of your QE labor, whether more or less than you expected, alleviates mental discord. A mind free of discord is capable of reflecting Eufeeling. And Eufeeling, as you now know, is necessary for healing to unfold.

It is far easier to start a QE session by letting your partner know that you cannot discern how much healing will result. You might say, "We will accept whatever we get." You should also mention that not everything will be immediately obvious, and healing may continue for several days after the session. Finally, you may want to add that improved results sometimes require additional QE sessions.

But before we continue, maybe I should take this opportunity to state the obvious: Quantum Entrainment can be used for any kind of healing and should always be performed in conjunction with, not instead of, qualified medical treatment. QE is a powerful adjunct to traditional health-care practices. It can only enhance the efforts of other healing systems, increasing the depth of healing and considerably shortening total healing time. Often, if QE is done before seeing the appropriate health-care practitioner, the symptoms will disappear. Even if symptoms abate, one should always consult professional help to be certain that there are no underlying etiologies or additional undiscovered problems.

The more you practice QE, the more healing will take place in your own life. Your growing familiarity with pure awareness will spill over into your everyday life, bringing a level of fulfillment undreamed of. Equipped with nothing more than your own awareness, no matter where you go, you can initiate a healing event.

As you continue to initiate Quantum Entrainment, you will luxuriate in the joy of helping others and receive their gratitude for sharing this simple, life-changing process. And you are just scratching the surface! Wait till you see what is to come.

CHAPTER 11

Remote QE

Remote QE is performing Quantum Entrainment on partners without touching them. You can do this from across a room or across the world. In quantum physics, this instantaneous interaction at a distance is called *entanglement.*However, entanglement cannot transmit information faster than light.

Tens of thousands of people around the world are performing QE on their friends, family members, and perfect strangers with great success just from reading the QE books like you are doing. Many of those people have read these words translated into their own language, and QE still works. As a matter of convenience, most of those QE sessions are done remotely; and those initiators, as you will soon discover, were able to do QE with ease. If you find Remote QE impossible to believe, don't worry about it. You will still be able to do it no matter what you think is or is not possible. Quantum Entrainment is a scientifically reproducible procedure. *It is real.* It does not need belief to work. And if you don't believe that, ask any pain-free pets if they were asked to believe in QE before they were healed.

How to Do Remote QE

Basically, you will triangulate as you have in the other forms of Quantum Entrainment. The steps are the same with some minor adaptations. We obviously have to compensate for the lack of a physical partner, but Remote QE is infinitely easier to learn than other activities where you need a partner. For some obscure reason, the tango comes to mind. Oh well . . . here are a few suggestions.

Use a Surrogate

A surrogate is a replacement, someone who takes the place of your partner. Any warm body will do—your spouse or kids, the paperboy, the guy in the next cubicle. Just perform Remote QE on the physically present surrogate as if your absent partner were standing right in front of you. Make sure that your intention includes the name, image, or idea of your missing partner.

You can also use a pet as a surrogate. Animals usually make good stand-ins because they don't ask questions. They are used to the strange behavior of their masters and will probably submit willingly as long as there is a snack waiting for them at the end of the session. Although admittedly it may take quick fingers and a box of Band-Aids if your only pet is a ravenous piranha, the upside is that the snack would be provided during the QE session rather than afterward.

A third kind of surrogate can be a doll or stuffed animal. Actually, you could even draw a picture on a piece of paper and use that. Or just write down your partner's name. All of these replacements will work just fine. Give it a try, and you will be pleasantly surprised.

Engage Your Imagination

If you have an active imagination, you can conjure up a mental image of your partner and triangulate it. Your fingers will not touch actual flesh, so you will have to imagine that, too. How do you know when to stop? You will feel the relaxation or melting under your imaginary fingers just as you do your physical ones.

Imagination QE can be done in a couple of ways. You can imagine that you are where your partner is. Visualize her sitting in her favorite chair while you apply Remote QE. Another option is to bring your partner to you. See her right there in front of you while you work your magic. Or you can meet anyplace you like. You are limited only by your imagination!

Try Air QE

You've heard of air guitar—pretending to hold the neck of an imaginary guitar while you pick, strum, and gyrate wildly in front of the mirror? Well, Air QE is a little like that. Standing or sitting, imagine your partner in front of you. Whether your eyes are open or closed is completely up to you. Now physically move your body and reach out your hands to place your fingers on your absent partner. You do everything as if your partner were there. Just don't let your spouse walk by unawares in the middle of the session. "Lucy, you got some splainin' to do!"

Remote QE is a wonderful way to get in all the QE practice you need. I do a session nightly before I go to bed. I usually have a list of people who have asked for help during the day. I also include partners who need continued care with chronic or life-threatening illnesses like Alzheimer's and cancer. Friends who at first thought regular Quantum Entrainment was weird now regularly call and ask for Remote QE.

With practice, you will soon be able to conduct Remote QE anytime there is a break in your day. I've even done it while partners were describing their problem to me. By the time they finished their explanation, the pain had disappeared. It is absolutely wonderful to be so close to the creative force and watch it work its wonders. Our only limits are our unaware minds—and Quantum Entrainment will fix that, too.

Self QE

Actually, you already know how to work the marvels of Quantum Entrainment on yourself. Just pick a method already described and apply it to yourself. If you have forgotten that you don't have to physically touch the afflicted area, then you will need to buy the home edition of *Twister: For Double-Jointed Yoga Masters* if you want to physically work on your back or other hard-to-reach places. So it is much easier if you remember you don't have to contact the affected area. If you have mid-back pain, for instance, you can triangulate on your knee or chest and be equally effective. Also consider using one of the Remote QE techniques previously mentioned.

Animals and Inanimate Objects

Because Quantum Entrainment draws from the most basic and all-permeating pure awareness, it should also work on animals and even inanimate objects. And it does! It's not all that strange when you think about it. We give medicines or chiropractic adjustments to our pets. But when it comes to so-called inanimate objects, I guess it is a bit of a stretch.

Even inanimate objects are vibrating with life on the subtlest level. Nothing is inanimate in the ultimate sense, and within the subtlest vibration exists its cause: pure awareness. So QE can have an effect on inanimate objects as many have found out to their great delight. If you have a dead car battery or a sputtering refrigerator, share a little QE with it. What have you got to lose? At the very least, you will repair your own frustration. Since your partner does not have to believe in this healing method to get results or to even know that you're conducting it, animals also respond beautifully to Quantum Entrainment. Apply QE to your pet's problems or even to pesky varmints such as overenthusiastic raccoons, overzealous ants, or bothersome bears.

Food offers another area of exploration for creative QEers. Consider entraining your groceries, water, and nutritional supplements. Your intention might be to potentiate the beneficial ingredients or remove toxins, as well as to improve digestion and assimilation before a meal is eaten. If you say grace before a meal, then add Quantum Entrainment at the end of your prayer.

Are you getting the idea? Do QE for anything and everything all day long. You will love how your environment responds to your kindness.

CHAPTER 12

Emotional QE

We have been focusing on applying Quantum Entrainment to physical conditions. As remarkable as that is, there's more. "Emotional QE" is a powerful tool for quieting psychological pain. Like physical disharmony, psychological discordance can be removed instantly. It may have its roots deeply embedded in what our mind perceives as the past. Quantum Entrainment does not recognize the past, or even the future. Both concepts are illusions and bind the mind to the ever-deepening spiral of entropy. In other words, the flow of time is created in the mind. This fixation on what was and what will be plants the seed for psychological disease, which can only germinate and flourish under the watchful eye of Father Time.

According to quantum physics, time does not flow. It is the sweep of our consciousness that creates the illusion of time. It is the illusion of time that creates suffering.

When we think about future events, we are moving forward in time. When we visit our memories, we are moving back in time. All this movement takes place in the mind. It exists nowhere else in this universe but in our minds. Even though it appears otherwise, our time, our future, and our past are not shared by anyone else.

Don't get me wrong—our lives exist, but not in the way we think they do. This mistaken identity causes an overwhelming suffering that only deepens with each generation.

Emotional QE stops the mind in its tracks and makes it pay attention to right now, robbing it of its preoccupation with the past and future, as well as of its guilt, anger, anxiety, and fear. When we do QE with psychological discord, we shine the bright light of pure awareness on it. Here we can observe the disharmonious emotions and events with healing calm and clarity. The movie of our life continues to unfold as before but without the influence of those hurtful, afflictive emotions.

How Emotional QE Works

Removing psychological pain is as easy as removing physical pain—perhaps easier. You don't have to know what is causing the emotional distress in your partners. In fact, I strongly recommend that you allow partners to keep their emotional concerns private. This practice is important in two ways. First, it affords your partners a level of privacy that may be welcome, especially if they don't know you well or if they just want to keep their inner life to themselves. Second, you are saved from having to deal with someone else's emotions, which can be draining on your own emotions. And at the very least, it will save you time.

Emotional QE is completely safe. It is not a therapy of any kind. It does not require analysis or training because the initiator does not do anything. Healing is accomplished by the partners bathing their emotional discord in the healing waters of pure awareness. The initiator just gets the process started—that's it. You do not have to muck around in a roiling sea of raw emotions. Leave that to the professionals.

Speaking of professionals, if you are a trained psychiatrist, psychologist, or psychotherapist, you can use Emotional QE with great effectiveness in your practice. You may consider doing Emotional QE right after your first pretesting. Many initial sources of distress may be eliminated with little effort, and you can then focus on what is left with more traditional techniques. Emotional QE will also work wonders for established patients. It can sometimes help break through long-standing blocks and will accelerate the healing process in general.

The healing that takes place through Emotional QE is permanent. Fear is the basal emotion from which all others are spawned. Fear is created when ego appears to split from pure awareness and takes on its individual identity. It does not matter if your partner is experiencing anger, anxiety, guilt, or sadness; at the bottom of it all is the fear of separation from pure awareness. Emotional QE floods fear with fullness, returning ego to awareness of pure awareness. The memory remains a ripple of awareness, but the debilitating emotion is merged into an ocean of bliss.

How to Apply Emotional QE

First let your partner know that you do not have to know about his psychological pain. Explain that it is pure awareness that does the healing, and you only get the process started. He can keep his emotional discord private.

Ask him to think about the incident that is creating the distress. If there is no clear incident, then have him privately identify the emotion. Encourage him to allow his emotions to grow stronger. When they can get no stronger, ask him to grade his emotional discomfort on a scale from one to ten (ten being unbearable). Remember his pretest number.

Proceed as you did when removing physical problems with QE. Here you can either do QE Triangulation or Refined QE.

When you have finished the session, give your partner some time to reorient. Emotional QE may sometimes require more time than QE applied to physical complaints. As soon as your partner is ready, have him bring up the same incident and once again assess its impact on a scale from one to ten.

At this point, partners usually express that they cannot even bring the emotion to mind! Or they will say something like, "I'm trying, but all I can get is a one or two." You can see that their facial muscles have relaxed, and there is serenity in their voice.

Emotional QE instantly removes uncomfortable emotions even when a person doesn't know why they are there. Pure awareness is able to get to the root without conscious awareness. On occasion, your partners may remember the offending event and mention it during the session. This is especially so when they discover a deeply buried childhood trauma. Don't put much emphasis on this. Ask them to remain silent and close their eyes if they like. The abhorrent emotion has already been neutralized by the time your partners have retrieved the memory, so there is no value in spending any more time on it.

You can feel content that you were able to inspire a healing of your partner's emotional conflict, and our troubled world is one candle brighter.

CHAPTER 13

Extended QE

Extended Quantum Entrainment is valuable for chronic, long-standing, or life-threatening health concerns such as diabetes, heart disease, Alzheimer's, or cancer. It is also especially effective at soothing and healing deep emotional conflicts. When a malady does not respond after several minutes or several attempts of regular QE sessions, then that partner is a candidate for Extended QE.

As the name implies, we are *extending* the usual time of QE, thus profoundly increasing the benefits to partner and initiator alike. Technically, any QE session that lasts more than five minutes is considered Extended QE. When it is performed, the common world of cars, stars, people, and even space becomes supersaturated in the depths of pure awareness. So much so that pure awareness becomes almost tangible, a healing salve of vibrant renewal.

Extended QE is remarkably powerful. And it is especially important to remember that pure awareness knows what needs to be done. Because it is human nature, we feel the need for stronger desire and more effort when working with life-threatening conditions. It is easy to forget that we are initiators where the intention for healing is already implied, and that is all. Healing will either take place or it won't—that is out of our hands. The severity of the condition does not call for stronger desire or more effort. Simple innocence is called for, and nothing more. That will get the job done.

How to Do Extended QE

An Extended QE session can last from five minutes to an hour or so. Twenty minutes seems about right for most of my sessions, although I will lengthen or shorten the time as needed.

Begin an Extended QE session exactly as you would a regular QE session of one or two minutes. I like to start out standing and then have my partner sit down a couple of minutes later. Extended QE can also be done lying down, especially if your partner is ill.

There are some minor differences with Extended QE that should be noted. To start, hold your contact points and wait for Eufeeling. As your Extended QE session continues, your mind will wander, and when you realize that it's elsewhere, just easily again become aware of Eufeeling. Your original Eufeeling will more than likely change. You may first experience stillness or peace that may give way to bliss, joy, or even ecstasy. Whatever Eufeeling is there, just be aware of it.

Every few minutes, when the notion strikes you, move your contact fingers to other parts of your partner's body. Common places for Extended QE are the forehead, temples, heart, and solar plexus, although any appropriate area of the body will do just fine. As soon as your fingers find their new position, return to your Eufeeling and settle in for the next few minutes.

Because of the longer time spent with Eufeeling, you may become sensitive to more refined levels of healing. You may perceive joints lubricating or lungs opening to receive life-giving air. You may see or feel other healing forces at work, too. Don't get involved. Whatever you view, just let it unfold on its own. You have a front-row seat as the healing impulses of pure awareness rise up and take form. You are the innocent observer to creation and re-creation. Nothing you do can improve on that. Know that this time is special, and you are blessed to be the silent witness.

You may also see geometric symbols or the flowing and swirling of abstract energies at work within you and your partner's body. The heavens may open and golden light may shower down upon you. Angels may sing and blow their trumpets to herald the coming healing. Your job? Just take it all in. Don't get caught up in the symbolism or symptomatology of it all. Just be there and enjoy the ever-growing healing presence of pure awareness.

When the Extended QE session is over, allow at least two or three minutes for your partners to open their eyes and return to regular activities. That is a minimum. They may need a full five or ten minutes, or to even lie down afterward. Make sure to let them know that if they get tired later in the day, they should rest and should also get a good night's sleep.

As with the shorter QE sessions, the healing that is started during Extended QE will continue for a day or two afterward. On occasion, your partner may feel tired or emotional the following day. This is an indication that very deep healing is taking place, and, if at all possible, your partner should rest, eat well, and do some light exercises.

I rely heavily on Extended QE in my counseling practice. It is a remarkably potent purifier of emotions and healer of the body. And, of course, I love it for what it does for me. I will continue to rely on it until I experience that final paradigm shift that allows me to walk through walls or float featherlike through the air.

Until that happens—and I'll certainly let you know when it does—it is Quantum Entrainment in all its variations for me.

PART II

EUFEELING, QE AWARENESS, AND QE INTENTION

CHAPTER 14

Who Am I? Finding Your Eternal Self

There is more to human development than we have been living. Innately we know that there must be something more to life. Maybe you have asked yourself that very question in a time of quiet desperation. It usually comes in midlife when we have acquired most of the things we desired, yet we feel an intangible emptiness, an inner incompleteness. The voice, no more than a gentle ripple across the ocean of the mind, issues from that strange, still place deep inside. We listen closely, for we know it is trying to tell us something important. But it is a frail voice drowned out by the wind and waves of daily living. And so we go on forging the life that our forefathers dreamed for us, the life of dominion over our environment, a life that ultimately reflects opulence, power, and pride.

We expect to find happiness like the fabled pot of gold at the end of the rainbow of our lives. Happiness in all its guises—relationships, sex, money, and more—is a phantom of reality. Once achieved it has no substance, no lasting value to give us what we really yearn for. That will only come with a clear and innocent perception of our true reality. The truth is that we are living half a life. We have not yet slipped into our spiritual skin. We have not grown into our full potential as dynamic, fun-loving paragons of peace and propriety.

We were born with everything we need to be free of the destructive tendencies of the immature adult.

I don't think there are many who would argue that we are capable of far more harmony and healing than we are presently exhibiting. I am not suggesting we try to overcome destructive tendencies, nor am I suggesting that we try to neutralize them with positive thoughts or actions. We have pursued both paths with little lasting success. I am suggesting that we don't try anything—in fact, trying will only make it worse.

It is achieved simply through a shift in perception. The child in us knows it instinctively. The adult only need accept that it is true, right here, right now. That is the elegant truth. But what is that perception, and how can we make it true for us?

No matter what your body-mind is experiencing, there has always been that part of you that remained separate and unchanged: the silent, eternal witness of your inner Self. That is the timeless You, the eternal Self, which will never leave you. How could it? You can leave your body and your mind, but you can never leave your Self.

Just the realization that there is something that is stable in life has a very settling effect. We feel somehow more secure knowing that there is a part of us that does not decay. We may not know how to explain it or show it to others, but we know it is there and that is enough for now.

But don't worry. You will soon learn how to make this experience vivid and vibrant in your life. Let's look a little more closely at what it means to live in this heightened state of awareness. Here is an experience that can break through the rigid thinking that imprisons the adult mind.

Experience: Finding Your Eternal Self

Evoke an early memory from childhood, perhaps one where you were playing quietly by yourself or some other pleasant activity. Now let you mind shift to an event later in your childhood. Choose events in adolescence, young adulthood, and continue to the present time. Let the memory become more vivid. Stay with each occurrence for as long as you like, remembering the sounds and smells, how your body felt, and what emotions were in your mind. When you finish with one memory, move to the next more recent memory.

After you have revisited several memories from different times in your life, let them all flow along in your mind at one time like a river. As you do so, realize that you are observing your memories. It is like you are on the bank of the river watching your memories flow by. Know that at this moment, you are the observer of what is occurring in your mind—in this case, your memories.

Go back to one of the single memory events you just had and remember it very clearly. As you watch your memory unfold, acknowledge that during the actual event, while you were making the memory, you also had a part of you that was watching what you were doing. There was a part of you that was observing even then. Visit another memory, and see that you were actually observing during that event as well.

Now take all the memories you chose earlier, and watch them from beginning to end in quick succession. Note that your body, intellect, emotions, desires, and skills all changed as you aged from childhood to adulthood. But there was something that didn't change. The sense of I, the silent witnessing Self, was always there just as it is right now. Become conscious that you are aware of it, aware of this whole process going on right now. Become aware that you were aware then and you are aware now. Know that there is nothing in that awareness but awareness: unchanging, undying awareness itself.

Most of us live in Newton's land of laws, the goal-oriented land of cause and effect. Convinced that when we perform X + Y, we would certainly achieve the target result Z. That is, we are certain that getting an education and a good job—while picking up a family, a house, and a dog along the way—will allow us to amass sufficient security and wealth to live out the rest of our lives in relative ease and happiness. How many of us are exactly where we planned to be ten years ago? It's almost impossible to get precisely what we plan for in life. Life has other plans for us. We strive for what we want, but life gives us what we need. Life offers us viable alternatives to our journey, and if we resist, life offers us obstacles.

When I refer to *life* here, I am talking about the natural laws to which we are all subservient: the laws that govern our species, our Earth, and even the vast worlds that revolve beyond our comprehension. And most of all, the law that underlies them all, the law of perfection through present perception. What does that mean? Don't let the words scare you off. It is quite straightforward. Present perception means becoming aware of pure awareness, a simple shift from common consciousness to unbounded awareness that anyone who is reading these lines can do effortlessly. It is the missing link that unites the freedom of childhood with the progressive power of adulthood.

Bear with me a little longer, and I will not only explain how it works but also how to win the favor of Mother Nature and live free from the binding influence of struggle and stress. Just know that when we bend or break the laws of nature we will be reprimanded. In childhood it is our mother who suggests, guides, and disciplines us. In adulthood Mother Nature takes over the job. As we already know, she can be brutal and unrelenting or compassionate, loving, and generous. The decision is not hers but ours to make.

This is not just some fanciful, pie-in-the-sky philosophy. What I am saying is as tangible as the air you are breathing. We have many examples of those who have lived this elevated human existence. It is not a matter of learning something new but more of remembering; remembering what we are, remembering our very essence. It is like returning to the freedom of childhood while living within the confines of control-oriented adulthood. It is a coming together of childhood and adulthood to form a new, exciting compilation of the best of both lives. It is a kind of enlightenment, an opening to the quiet power that lies within each and every one of us.

CHAPTER 15

How to Find Nothing

Humans—that means you and me—are meant to be free and fun loving. We have all the equipment it takes, but it seems we're looking down the barrel of the gun rather than the sights. We've got our lives turned around by placing value on the fruits of our labor and little on the organizing influence behind it.

In Chapter 4 ("Stopping Your Thoughts—It's Easy!"), you sat down, closed your eyes, and asked yourself a question after which you waited to see what would happen. While you were waiting, you realized that nothing was happening—that your thoughts had stopped, and you were enjoying the total piece of non-activity. You discovered pure awareness waiting for you between your thoughts. If pure awareness truly is everywhere all the time, then it must be right here, right now. You should be able to become aware of pure awareness with your eyes open while you are reading this book or doing anything else. This next experience will show you how to do just that. It is so simple and so immediate that you will wonder how you could possibly have missed it all these years.

> *Turn your head all the way to your left, and look at an object.*
> *Now quickly turn your head all the way to your right, and look at another object.*

What was in your mind while your head was turning from the first object to the second object? Nothing, right? Your mind was completely blank. Do it again and again if you like. The result will always be the same . . . nothing!

You have already learned that nothing is pure awareness and that pure awareness is your basic nature. Everything you know and experience is founded on pure awareness. Buddha put it this way: "To see nothing is to perceive the Way." The Beatles said, "Nothing's gonna change my world." And Frank says, "There's nothing to it." What do we mean?

When you become aware of a tree, the impression it makes in your mind is projected onto the screen of pure awareness. That is what we call a thought. In this case, it is a thought about the tree. It is not the tree itself, right? This thought of the tree is imprinted on pure awareness like a movie is imprinted on the screen at the front of the theater. The screen was always there, and the movie didn't start until the images were projected on the screen. It is the same with your mind. Living doesn't start until the images of life—the thoughts, emotions, and perceptions from the outside world—are projected on the screen of your mind: pure awareness.

The problem comes when you forget pure awareness and believe that the images projected in your mind are real—thinking that the tree in your mind is an accurate representation of the real tree in your backyard. That would be like going to a movie and believing you are a character being projected on the screen. When you believe you are part of the movie, you weep and laugh, fall in and out of love, and experience all the drama the film has to offer. Behind it all, supporting all the images of the movie, is the screen. Without it, there would be no movie. As a moviegoer, you already know this. But as a person living in your mind, you have forgotten that all the images of your life could not exist if they were not reflected on pure awareness, the screen of your mind.

When you are aware of pure awareness, you are aware of your basic nature, which is unbounded and unchanging. When you are aware of pure awareness you are secure. When you become aware of pure awareness you are a cosmic sponge soaking up the expansive stability, strength, peace, and joy of pure awareness. Soon and without effort, emotional and mental discord begin to melt into the vastness of your Self. You draw from the peace and harmony and absolute stability that pure awareness is, and your life becomes a reflection of those qualities. When you are not aware of pure awareness . . . well, you already know how that feels.

Aware of Pure Awareness → Unwavering Security →
Healthy Emotion → Clear Thinking → Dynamic Action

Becoming aware of pure awareness is a great adventure, but there is more. And now we come to the main focus of Quantum Entrainment, Eufeeling, and what it will bring to your life. Simply put, Eufeeling will fulfill your deepest desire. That's right—the deepest, most desperate desire, hiding in the deepest, most desolate part of your mind, will be fulfilled when you come to know Eufeeling. Not bad for starters, wouldn't you say? But here's the really neat thing. Anyone can easily experience Eufeeling, and that means you. You don't have to take my word for it, for shortly you will prove it to yourself.

Not to get too far ahead of myself, but I'm excited to share this with you; and after you and Eufeeling become old buddies, I have another surprise for you. I want you to learn how to rewrite the movie that is your life. After Eufeeling is established in your awareness, you will learn how to begin to get the things you want from life: more money, deeper relationships, a more fulfilling job, the ability to travel, more free time, and, most important, more fun. But before we change your world from the inside out, let's take a few minutes to learn more about Eufeeling and how it works the wonders it performs.

I have worked hard all of my adult life. I worked especially hard at becoming enlightened. To me, enlightenment was a state of eternal happiness. In my mind, I had this utopian idea that when I was enlightened, I would walk on a cloud of bliss looking down on the suffering masses and saying to myself, *Tsk, tsk. Look at all those suffering people down there. I sure am glad that I'm above it all.*

Enlightenment became my goal, and I had a burning desire to reach that goal as quickly as possible. Little did I know that the very desire that put me on the path to freedom actually imprisoned me in a never-ending labyrinth that continually turned back upon itself. Desire is Ouroboros, the snake that swallows its own tail. When desire is done with you, there is nothing left, which, if you can accept it, is a good thing. Nothing is the beginning and the end of the path. It also happens to be the middle as well, but few recognize it as so.

Here's a tip: Whenever you are on a path to find unbounded bliss and eternal freedom, get off that path immediately. If something is unbounded and eternal, then it must already be where you are. You don't need a path to get you where you already are because you are already there. Does that make sense? Stop making effort, and peace will be waiting for you like stillness after a violent storm. The best time for you to realize your material goals is not while you are being buffeted by the tempest of trepidation but after the storm clouds have exhausted themselves. In the sunshine of a new day, you will build upon the foundation of Eufeeling and quickly realize the peace and prosperity that is patiently waiting for you.

CHAPTER 16

How to Find More Nothing

Begin to perform a simple action such as putting down the book you are reading or walking across the room. Any simple activity will do. Somewhere during the act, suddenly stop moving. Now pay attention to what is in your mind. Then focus on what your body is feeling.

When you stop in the middle of any action, you will find your mind empty and your body still. No matter where you are or what you are doing, be it a single action or your life's journey, *nothing* is always there with you . . . always!

You need a path for relative things like finding the grocery store and achieving financial security. Paths are necessary to reach out for and find the relative things in our lives. But when it comes to securing something that is everywhere all the time—like pure awareness and Eufeeling—a path is pretty much useless. Actually, it is worse than use-less. It's a waste of life.

You can't get something you already have no mat-ter how hard you try. If you believe there is a path to unbounded love, then your belief is blinding you. You can't see the forest for the trees. You can try and try and try, cre-ating great effort for many years, and you will still not be able to get what you already have. How do I know? Because I already tried and tried and tried.

One time I quit trying and felt so good that I thought, *If not trying makes me feel so good, then imagine how much peace I can get if I really worked it.* Do you see the lunacy in this thinking? Peace comes from less activity, not more. Our peaceful moments don't come while we're multitask-ing. They come when our mind is at rest. If I would have stayed in the stop-trying mode, peace would have been permanent—instead, I tried and tried and tried some more.

This is a common mistake. Once we reach a goal, once we get something we've worked hard for, we feel pretty good. We think we feel good because we got what we wanted. In reality, the deeper, inner good feeling comes because we don't have to try to get that thing anymore. There is a little space of complete non-doing, and it is filled with joy or peace or a sense of satisfaction. Because we misunderstand the nature of peace, we try to fill that space with more activity. Soon after we reach a goal, we start to feel antsy and immediately turn to find another mountain to climb.

Sometimes we can't even enjoy our moment of stillness because our mind is already looking ahead to the next con-quest. It knows that happiness is fleeting. The mind is ever searching for that permanent happiness, and this is where Eufeeling comes in.

Eufeeling is everywhere all the time. That's why I've said that it has always been with you. If Eufeeling is there with you right now and you are not aware of it, then where should you go, and what should you do to find it? The incredibly simple answer is that there is nowhere to go and nothing to do except *become aware of it.* And how should you become aware of it? The answer is without trying and creating effort. This is the secret, the key to unlock the amulet of suffering you've been carrying around your neck since you left your childhood behind. Stop trying.

CHAPTER 17

How to Perceive
Without Effort

Think of a number from one to ten. Next picture a color in your mind. Finally, think of a tall tree. Now, one right after the other, think of the number, the color, and the tree.

When you thought of the number and then thought of the color, how hard was it for your mind to go from one to the other? Did you say, *Okay mind, let's think of the number. And now that we have the number in mind, let's work our way over to think about the color. We have the color firmly in mind now, so let's go over and think about the tree.* Of course your mind doesn't work this way at all. It moved automatically and without effort from one object to the other. The whole process was effortless.

Now this exercise is a little misleading because it doesn't teach you how to perceive without effort. You already do that. The real value of this exercise is to make you consciously aware of how effortless the process of perceiving is. Any trying on your part would only get in the way.

So what have we learned so far? For starters, Eufeeling is unbounded, and because it is everywhere, it has always been with us. Regular emotions like anger and anxiety are not unbounded. They are bound to our past and future, to our memories, our hopes, and our fears. The flavor and intensity of our emotions depends on how secure we feel at any given moment. We can be tossed about by the waves of emotions like a rudderless ship on a stormy ocean. Or we can anchor to the stability of Eufeeling resulting in inner peace, joy, and love. We don't have to do anything to become aware of Eufeeling except to perceive it. Perceiving is effortless; therefore, perceiving Eufeeling is effortless.

So you might say, "If perceiving Eufeeling is so effortless, how come I haven't been able to perceive it?" Yes, perceiving is effortless, but it is like the beam of a flashlight. You just point the beam at what you want to observe and, presto, you see the illuminated object glowing in your awareness. But no matter how effortless the process is, if you point the flashlight in the wrong direction, you will never find what you are looking for. The only reason Eufeeling eludes you is because you are looking in the wrong direction. Once you learn how to find Eufeeling, that is the direction in which you must turn in order to perceive it. You will never lose it again. It is my job to turn you in the right direction and then step out of the way while you and Eufeeling get to know each other.

In case you are having a bit of difficulty locating Eufeeling intellectually, I have drawn a little illustration for you.

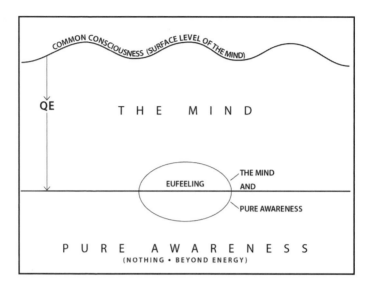

As you can see, QE takes our awareness from common consciousness to pure awareness beyond the mind. Eufeeling exists both in pure awareness and in the created world, here depicted as the mind. Eufeeling is the only "thing" in creation that is both unbounded and created. When you become aware of Eufeeling, you're able to think and act from that most rarified and harmonious level of thinking. That means your every thought, word, and action is more harmonious and orderly, opening it to the greatest potential of fulfillment on the material level. Now let's explore further how Eufeeling awareness creates maximum health, prosperity, and love in our life.

CHAPTER 18

Bringing Eufeeling into Your World

By uncovering Eufeeling within you, you have discovered the pivot point around which all life revolves. When you become aware of Eufeeling, your life becomes anchored in the unshakable, unbounded essence of creation beyond the touch of time. Without awareness of Eufeeling, life is unbalanced, but this is no longer your concern, at least personally. Now that you are among the newly awakened, there is no time to sit around on your laurels. Yes, the perception of Eufeeling is effortless, but unless you plan to live in a cave, you must take a little time to integrate Eufeeling into your daily activity.

When you learned QE, you learned to go beyond mental and emotional activity into pure awareness. Then instead of forgetting about pure awareness and returning to the relative world, you learned to perceive Eufeeling, which anchors your awareness at the deepest, most silent level of your mind where thoughts are created. Sitting, settled in the bliss of Eufeeling, you actually become a witness to creation. As soon as you are comfortable with your role as witness, you will learn how to create from that most subtle and powerful level of life deep within the mind. This process of creating power and grace in your life, not to mention wealth and wellness, is called QE Intention. Once you learn QE Intention, you will become the master of your own creation, and you won't have to do a thing.

You will learn non-doing and from there be able to satisfy your desires. You will set potent forces in motion that will form around those desires to manifest them on the material plane. You will learn how to use QE Intention for financial freedom, emotional management, problem solving, chronic health issues, and most important, how to help others realize their heart's desires.

I am a great fan of simplifying things. Everywhere I look, I see people working harder and getting less done. The increased quantity and diminished quality of work seems to be directly proportional to the amount of multitasking one can do. There is a movement afoot in business to do less and get more done. Oddly enough, I see people working very hard to accomplish this. It is the nature of the unanchored mind, the active mind of modern living, to do more and more, looking for the ultimate solution. Paradoxically, it is the still mind anchored in the deep harmony of inner peace that has found a solution. The mantra of the QE mind is, "Do nothing and achieve everything." Once you become comfortable hanging out at the bottom of your mind, then you will learn QE Intention: how to get everything by doing nothing.

You really can't "use" Eufeeling, but you can become aware of it in various situations and watch how it enriches the quality of life for you and those around you. It truly is a most amazing process. At first your mind will want to roll up its sleeves and get to work on the business of creation. Ego can be heard to say, "I can do great things and even manifest lots of cool material stuff in my life." This motivation is driven by the need to show some value and create some effect in one's world, but that's just the ego wanting to strut its stuff. Very quickly ego will see the sense of letting go, letting nature—or, in this case, Eufeeling—take its course. Quickly it will become crystal clear that creation has gotten along perfectly well up to now without any help from your ego. Soon the burden of "I am the creator" falls gently from your shoulders like a worn-out garment to be replaced by the realization, "I am the observer through which creation unfolds."

So I'm not going to emphasize the outward stroke of creation as I have in previous works. Instead, you will learn to settle into the profound silence of Self and from that exalted seat secretly conceal a seed whose blossom will be the thousand-petaled lotus of your life. Then inner fulfillment will be reflected in every aspect of your life . . . and you can also manifest lots of cool material stuff! So let's move along to the next step of creating inner peace and outer abundance. You can begin by becoming aware of Eufeeling while doing quieter, less hectic activities. You can start by sitting in a chair and performing the next exercise.

Sitting with Eufeeling

Find a comfortable chair where you won't be bothered for at least 15 minutes. Turn off the phone, usher the pets from the room, close the door, and settle comfortably into your chair. Do Refined QE (Chapter 9). After you have walked around the room quietly identifying Eufeeling in the objects around you, return to your seat and close your eyes. Now continue Refined QE, and once again become aware of your Eufeeling. Do this for five minutes.

After five minutes or so, slowly move one of your fingers, and then immediately become aware of Eufeeling for five to ten seconds. Next move your whole hand, and then return to Eufeeling for another five to ten seconds. Repeat this process with other parts of your body, remembering to move that part of the body and then return to Eufeeling. For example, you could go from your hand, to your nose, to your left eye, to your right knee, and then to the hair on your head. Where you go or in what order is not important. Just remember to physically move that area, and then become aware of Eufeeling for five to ten seconds afterward. Now finish off with another three to five minutes of QE, the innocent awareness of Eufeeling.

I would like you to do the Sitting with Eufeeling exercise two to four times a day. Ideally, they would be 15-minute sessions each, but they don't have to be. If you do three or four sessions of five minutes each, that will be just fine. Do what you can, but be diligent about committing to this practice every day for the next three or four days. It is important that you establish a very solid foundation of QE Awareness on which to build QE Intention. Review the instructions on how to do QE at least once a day to make sure you don't pick up any bad habits. You want to take every opportunity to spend time with Eufeeling at the bottom of your mind. It is from this level of awareness that you will create your life anew.

You don't have to restrict yourself to just sitting. Whenever you think of it—driving your car, talking with a co-worker, brushing your teeth, or any other activity—become aware of Eufeeling and the deep stillness that accompanies it. Allow this to be an enjoyable activity, not a chore. You will quickly find your mind automatically going to Eufeeling when the opportunity presents itself. Just go with the flow, reminding yourself to check in with Eufeeling whenever you think of it. You may be aware of it for a few minutes or a few seconds; it doesn't matter at this point. Keep in mind the saying: *If it isn't easy and it isn't fun, it isn't QE.*

As you're becoming more in tune with the peaceful, unbounded nature of Eufeeling and confirming the quiet command of QE Awareness in your daily routine, I have a few more things I would like to discuss. I would especially like to take a closer look at the mind, ego, desire, and the mechanics of suffering. I think you will find it fascinating dialogue, and I'm anxious to tell you all about it. So hold on to your hat. We are off and running.

CHAPTER 19

The Solution to Suffering

Ah, desire! How the mind lights up when it hears that word. Desire excites the imagination and prepares the body for pleasure. Desire creates a spur to action. It is the quest to fulfill desire that drives humankind to delve into the deepest waters, ascend the highest peaks, and dream beyond the stars. Desire is the great motivator and the cause of many sleepless nights. Driven by desire, we launch wars, cure diseases, build societies, and explore the depths of the human soul.

Desire is both a boon and a bane: a boon when it is satisfied, and a bane when it isn't. All life moves away from pain and toward pleasure. It is desire that provides both the inspiration and motivation to move beyond our limitations and fill our greatest potential.

The spectrum of desire can range from a light tickle in the back of our minds to an overwhelming obsession that drives us to destruction. Before we go a step further, let's do a little experiment to help us better understand how desire, the emotions attached to an impulse, affects us emotionally.

The Solution to Suffering (Losing Desire)

After reading this exercise, lay down your book, close your eyes, and follow the instructions.

With eyes closed, think about something that you really, really want—something that you desire with all your heart. Note how you feel when you think about the possibility of getting this object of desire. You might feel excitement or hope or even nervousness about obtaining it. Take a moment to register your feelings.

Now imagine that you actually have gotten what you desire, and note how your feelings change. Your anticipation and hopefulness may be replaced with the joy of achievement or contentment or even pride. You see that there is a shift in the kind and quality of your emotions.

Next imagine that what you have is abruptly taken away from you. How do you feel when you lose what you had? Your emotions most probably take a turn toward the negative. You may feel a sense of loss or sorrow, or perhaps frustration and even anger.

What does this simple exercise teach us? Something that, when observed on the surface, seems obvious and even innocent can be quite alarming once we take a more discerning look. On the surface, we recognize that emotions accompany desire and that our emotions change with the circumstances. They are different when we want something, different still when we get something, and change again when we lose something. But hidden beneath the obvious is something much more sinister, which, we will find out, is the cause of underlying restlessness, worry, and chronic dissatisfaction. We're about to discover the secret of suffering, the seed of disharmony and discontent.

We have traditionally taken this approach. That is, we feel the need to reach out and pluck the object of our desire for our very own. We overcome the various elements standing in our way and then feel the exuberant joy of finally reaching the goal or owning the object. That seems logical. Just get what you want and eliminate the pricking of that uncomfortable thorn we call desire. Unfortunately, securing the object is only a temporary fix. As soon as one desire is quelled, another rises to take its place. Isn't that true? After a brief interlude where we feel a kind of relative quiet—a mellow satisfaction in our minds—we again become restless and are soon off on another quest to quell desire.

In affluent countries, many if not most of our desires are for things we want but do not absolutely need. Think about it. Do we really need a quadruple-bladed razor; a 52-inch TV; designer jeans; 12 pairs of shoes (I'm being very conservative here—some individuals amass scores of pairs of shoes . . . you know who you are); a shiny red sports car; or a double mocha latte with an extra shot of decaf espresso, whipped cream, and chocolate sprinkles? If you doubt me, take a quick look in your closet, kitchen, or garage and note all the items lying about that you desired, obtained, and are now not using. Some may still have the price tag on them. Our common experience is that shortly after we satisfy our craving for an object, it loses its appeal. We can desire things that we need and things that we don't need—that's obvious. The fruits of life are meant to be eaten. Who doesn't feel better watching a little TV, wearing new clothes, or going out to dinner with friends? It is not the usefulness of a desire that we are concerned with here. What is more important is why a desire forms and if it can be satisfied in a more practical, even more prevailing way.

It appears that the object has the power to remove desire, but upon closer inspection, we find that this simply is not true. Well, forgive me. It's true in a superficial sense. But there seems to be a deeper underlying desire from which we are never completely liberated. That desire is the source, the progenitor of all other desires. That basic desire is the head of Medusa, the mythological monster with snakes for hair, who turns you to stone by only looking in your eyes. The lesser desires are the snakes wriggling and writhing, hard to grab and harder to hold. Cut off the head of one snake, as the fable goes, and two more take its place. You have probably noticed this in your own life: satisfy one desire, and two more take its place. The only way to completely rid yourself of all those pesky varmints is to cut off the head of Medusa. Following through with our analogy, this would mean finding and fulfilling that deepest, most basic desire.

When we acquire the object of desire, we retire the fire of desire. (Hey, I made it rhyme! I just love poetry, don't you?) We look at the object as if it has the power to put out that fire. The object becomes the focus of our efforts, and if not consciously, certainly subconsciously, it is elevated to the exalted position of desire slayer. But that is all illusion.

Have you ever noticed that as soon as you reach a goal—get a raise, buy a house, win an award, or fall in romantic love—the good feeling just doesn't last? Why is that? Why can't we stay satisfied for long? Objects, people, organizations, philosophies, and dreams are a relative fascination. They are Medusa's mesmerizing snakes distracting our mind from the reality of life. Most people go from one thing to another all their lives searching for that ultimate happiness. When we are driven by desire, we can never rest; that is, until we die. Outward goals lead away from inner peace, which is why we fail to find lasting satisfaction in relative matters. We are meant to realize the ultimate matter, as it were: Eufeeling. Eufeeling is the ultimate goal. It brings with it the dissolution of desire as a motivating entity. Eufeeling is the death of desire.

Okay, I can't help myself. I have to take the Medusa analogy a little further. As the story goes, Perseus beheaded Medusa. He grabbed her head by the snake-hair and held it up. Oddly enough, the snakes don't die, but they are unable to harm him. When we are aware of Eufeeling, we still have desires, but they cannot grab hold of us; they cannot constrict our mind with harmful emotions. What we want ultimately is to be at peace, free to sail the ocean of universal love without being buffeted by constant waves of desires. We want to be free of the desire for love. We want to love just for the sake of love. We want to be free of reason or circumstance or need. When living in QE Awareness, desires are no more than delightful dalliances, gentle ripples on the vast ocean of bliss we call Eufeeling. There we can love a leaf and a rock and a person all with the same intensity. In QE Awareness we look Medusa squarely in the eyes and know that universal love abides where fear once lived.

When we are aware of Eufeeling, the fulfillment of one desire doesn't create a desire for more. You already have more than most when you are aware of Eufeeling. QE Awareness breaks the desire-action-desire cycle because it satisfies the primal desire to feel whole and beyond harm.

Now the desire for a red sports car is just a blip on your emotional radar screen, a ripple on the ocean of wholeness. If you own unbounded wholeness, then owning a sports car is really a minor matter. After the initial desire-ripple passes, the ocean of wholeness remains still. Let's create a simple experience to emphasize this point.

Losing Desire, Continued

Imagine that you can create anything you want, anytime and in unlimited quantities. Visualize yourself getting all the things you have ever desired: food, money, friends, possessions, respect. Take time to develop a strong image, feeling emotions and using sight, smell, touch, hearing, and taste around the things you create.

Now that you can have anything you want, give it all away. Give it to poor people, friends, rich people, your teacher, your mother, your child, and so forth. Giving away what you have is easy because you know you can imagine more. It is not only easy to give when you have an unlimited supply, but it's also fun. It feels good. Giving from infinite resources frees you from the need to hold on. It liberates you from the feeling of deficiency and need and the desires they draw to them.

Every created thing enters this world through Eufeeling. If there were ever a field of infinite resources, then Eufeeling is it. Become aware of Eufeeling in just the right way, and all the forces of creation will mobilize on your behalf. This is what I call QE Intention. When you have a QE Intention, you become aware of the unbounded fullness that you are.

Your desires are tenderly hushed like crying babes in the arms of mother Eufeeling. Then the unbounded organizing influence of Eufeeling begins to bring order to your life. In complete harmony and free from the chaos of so many distracting desires, you will come to realize great satisfaction on the material plane as well.

QE Intention is natural. It is the way we were meant to be, free to enjoy the fullness of our bountiful world. Before we learn how to have a QE Intention, it will be good to get a bit of a deeper understanding of how it works. In the next chapter, you will be introduced to the forces that come into play to support your wishes and fulfill your deepest desires. In the meantime, continue to do Quantum Entrainment on a regular basis and slip into QE Awareness as often as feels comfortable throughout the day. As you bring together your experience and your understanding of Eufeeling, you're preparing your mind to revel in the delicate, delicious joys of the QE Intention.

CHAPTER 20

How to Have a QE Intention

There is a variation of being aware of Eufeeling. It is a very subtle perception of Eufeeling called *Pure Eufeeling*. This state is characterized by awareness of no thoughts but shouldn't be confused with pure awareness. When you are experiencing pure awareness, you are not aware of it at the time. It is a non-experience, or lack of experience. You only know that you were in pure awareness after your mind starts thinking again. You recognize it as a gap in your thinking, a period of non-experience.

Pure Eufeeling is the most refined awareness you can have. It is a perception of pure awareness and Eufeeling simultaneously. Pure Eufeeling means that you are perceiving Eufeeling before it reflects any form or feelings—like joy, peace, or bliss—in your mind. I only mention it here because you might confuse it with the non-thinking pure awareness state. You can tell Pure Eufeeling from pure awareness because you are aware of it at the time you are experiencing it. You know you are aware, but what you are aware of is nothing.

- *Pure Eufeeling:* Aware that you are aware of nothing while you are having it
- *Pure Awareness:* Not aware until you start thinking again, and you realize that there was a "gap" in your thinking

Either experience is not a goal. When you have Pure Eufeeling, you have no goals, only observation of what is reflecting in your mind. For what we are doing now, it doesn't matter whether you are aware of thoughts, Eufeeling, or pure awareness. Your interaction is still the same, innocent observation of the remarkable machinery of creation as it unfolds on the screen of Pure Eufeeling.

Pure Eufeeling is the most pure perception. There is no distortion, no ego to disrupt the clean expression of this impulse of purity. In common consciousness, your thoughts are like waves dashed on the rocky shores of reality exploding in a spray of chaos and criticism driven before the prevailing winds of cause and effect. On the deepest level of your mind, no such conflict can exist. So when you have a thought or a desire, it is immediately fulfilled. This is most amazing! You can have anything you want while you're experiencing Pure Eufeeling.

It is awareness at the Pure Eufeeling level that makes you the creator of your life—or more accurately, you become the primal witness beyond the will of ego. Here you are simultaneously the creator, the creation, and the unbounded awareness within and beyond both. It is from this level of awareness that you create miracles in your life. From Pure Eufeeling you will quell the anxiety and frustration of financial difficulties, resolve the anger and mistrust in relationships, and open your eyes to your inner power that has been, up to now, beleaguered by the rumble and rubble of your runaway mind. It is from this marvelous level of awareness that all life is renewed every instant of every day. Your life is no different.

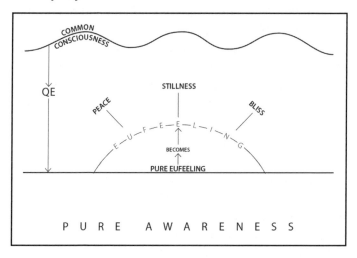

When you experience Pure Eufeeling, you are at once the creator and beyond creation. I know, I know . . . it doesn't seem to make sense. The mind functions in the field of form and cannot comprehend the formless. Your mind will never wrap itself around this reality, but you can have a knowing, an intuition that goes beyond understanding. To your mind, it's a paradox. How can you be both unbounded awareness and bound by thoughts and things? Your mind tells the only story it knows. But remember, you're not your mind. You are pure awareness, the space between the thoughts that fill your mind. There is only one creation. However, when it is viewed through an individual body-mind, all of creation is narrowed down to the individual and is seen as your life. Pure Eufeeling raises you to your unbounded status of the observer-creator so that you can enjoy the best of both worlds.

This is a very important realization. What does observer-creator mean? It means that you can change your life, create it anew, and, at the same time, not get caught in the often-debilitating wash of emotions and desires that accompany efforts to control life through common conscious. It means that you no longer have to create great effort to find success; you are free to languish in the joy of being fully human. In just a few moments, you're going to learn QE Intention, the technology of effortless fulfillment. You will learn to be successful on every level of your life, and the beauty of QE intention is that you don't need to understand a single thing that we have just been talking about. Talking and thinking are mental functions relegated to our process-bound minds. QE Intention will still work wonders for you even if you don't have a clue as to how it works. Fortunately, you don't have to take my word for it. It will work even if you don't believe in it. In a few short pages, you will prove it to yourself.

Receive Without Resistance

QE Intention is a reproducible, scientific process so simple that you can't fail. You will be in complete control when you become the silent witness, uninvolved in what you create. I know it sounds contradictory, but that doesn't matter. QE Intention will work for you regardless of what your mind thinks. You will have absolute control over your life as long as what you want to create will cause no harm. We all live under the universal influence of cause and effect, and trying to bend those laws in our favor never turns out to our complete benefit. When having a QE Intention, you, your loved ones, and the rest of the world are protected from wrong thinking and injurious action. When experiencing Pure Eufeeling, you can do no harm. If you want something that is supported by the laws of Nature, you will get it. It is just that simple. But listen to this: if you want something that isn't right for you, then something greater will be offered in its place. When Mother Nature's children awaken from the ego dreams of everyday living, she offers them her greatest gifts. She will oversee the unfolding of the laws of cause and effect on your behalf. When you do QE Intention, you may want a bicycle and end up with a BMW. All you need do is desire and sit back and wait.

QE Intention will prepare you to receive what is offered without resistance. You will be guided to greater success than you anticipate when you let the natural flow of creation lead you. You will naturally let go of your attachment to a path or idea or object when it will create more trouble than it is worth. In other words, from your private position at the heart of creation, you will be the first one to know if something will work or not. You will be the first to hear the gentle urgings from the silent space beyond your mind. You will be the first to enjoy the fruits of your non-labor completely accepting what is, as it is.

QE Intention is the vital element in any intention work. The further away from Eufeeling one tries to create success, the harder one must work. Intention work should be effortless. This is especially true when you would like to manifest your desires on the material plane. The further you are from the absolute organizing harmony of Pure Eufeeling, the more rules you will have to follow and the more detailed your intention must become. Traditional intention work can require a good bit of effort, detail, and repetition If you want a new home, you may be asked to build it in your mind. You may be told to create it brick by brick down to the color and position of every light switch, electric outlet, and cabinet handle. This method infers that the more detailed you are, the more the image is burned into your mind, and the better your chances of owning that new home will be. There may be many rules attached to your practice of intention. You might be asked to create your intention in a positive frame of mind. You may be asked to refer to the goal as if you have already achieved it. You may be encouraged to repeat your intention as often as you can think about it.

These practices that entail repetition and minute detail are many times successful but rarely for the reason we think. We know that it is the infinite organizing power of Pure Eufeeling that manifests our dreams and fulfills our deepest desires. When the mind is wrapped up in infinite detail or continuous repetition, it sometimes automatically slips into a deeper state of stillness within the mind. It does so despite the incessant activity around manifesting the intention. In this way, the intention becomes almost like a mantra actively entraining the mind until it fatigues. If the mind is sufficiently rested, it will dip into some of the quieter levels of mind. There the seed will be planted and begin to grow toward fruition. If the mind is tired, it will wander off to seek more interesting subject matter to explore, or it will just fall asleep.

It depends how deeply the intention seed was planted in the quieter regions of your mind as to how quickly and completely you will see results. Some people are naturally more inclined to access these quiet levels and are able to plant their intention seeds deeper. These people are the ones whose intentions seem to work for them much of the time. If you're not able to quiet your mind, you can do exactly as those who are successful and still not see results. It can be very frustrating and raise doubts as to whether you are worthy of getting what you desire. This is not the case at all. It is not the intention, nor the process, or even the person that meets with failure.

A successful intention relies on only one thing: the level of awareness. The deepest level of awareness you can experience is Pure Eufeeling. So you could say that the effectiveness of your intention depends on the quality of your awareness. With little practice and less effort, every man and woman can learn to greatly improve the quality of their awareness and therefore the effectiveness of their intention work.

As you will soon find out, QE Intention requires no more effort than the slightest mental impulse to realize fruition of your greatest hopes and goals. You don't have to give up what you are doing right now. That's right. You can continue to do your intention work as you always have with one single—and I might add, profound—addition. Instead of just thinking your intention or throwing in a little feeling to give it some emotional oomph, simply sink into the silent depths of your mind, the realm of infinite possibilities. You only have to add Pure Eufeeling to your intention work, and the improvement will be noticeable immediately.

One more thing before you learn how to have a QE Intention. Every intention has two parts to it: the object of the intention and the emotion that you attach to the intention. The object may be corporeal like trees and keys and bumblebee's knees, or a car or a house. An object can also be less concrete like higher education, a more compatible relationship, or greater spiritual harmony. The emotion attached to any intention usually springs out of a concern or fear that you will not get, or do not deserve, what you are asking for. For instance, you may apply for a new job that you really need. This is the object of your intention, and you may be very anxious about whether you will get it or not. Your anxiety is the emotion attached to the intention and has grown out of a fear that you will not get the job. In many cases, if not most, the emotion can be more debilitating and cause more discomfort than not getting what you desire.

Your worry about getting the job can interfere with actually getting the job. For instance, you can be the perfect candidate for the job but become so nervous that you fail the interview, and the job goes to a less-qualified candidate. The first thing that QE Intention does is to remove the emotional discord attached to achieving your goal. The quelling of the emotional disharmony does not take weeks or days or even hours. QE Intention immediately dissolves emotional discord so that all the creative energies can be focused on acquiring the goal. If eliminating emotional upset were the only thing you learned, it would be worth the price of this book a thousand times over. But there is more . . . much, much more.

Some systems of intention work actually encourage the addition of emotion to add momentum. Adding this kind of positive emotion to intention can have a stimulating effect. It can move us more quickly down the road to completion, but the emotion is the driving force not the guiding force.

When you have a QE Intention, you cannot take yourself in the wrong direction because you do nothing. You are just an observer along for the ride. The QE Intention elicits a delicate impulse completely revealing what you want. How and when you get it is completely up to the forces of creation. Eufeeling is the mastermind that organizes those forces on your behalf. You will not need to try and convince yourself of anything, nor will you need to put energy into creating a positive atmosphere. It will all flow from you as naturally as water flows down hill. Your delicate desire is enough to place you in the flow of the forces of creation, not to help you in your effort but to carry you beyond effort to the successful realization of your desire. You become the witness to your own creation, the progenitor of peace and harmony, with nothing more than a single thought.

The procedure you are about to learn is a technology from a far more simple time when we were more at home with our Self. It is a simple and yet an ultimately prevailing technology, which will return to us that which we lost out of ignorance and inattentiveness. We have discussed a lot in preparation for this time, but in the end QE Intention is a personal and intimate celebration of your Self. Its magic will still enfold you even if you understand nothing of what we have discussed. So lay down your analytical tools if you like, and prepare to return to the primal state before it was imposed upon by the mayhem of the modern mind.

A QE Intention session is a specific, well-defined event, at least in the beginning. In time your QE Intention session will start and finish in the blink of an eye. It will require no preparation. But for now, we will go through the process step-by-step, ensuring that it becomes second nature for you. In a very short time, having a QE Intention will be as natural as thinking.

Now please pay special attention to the following, as it is crucial to the successful execution of QE Intention. QE Intention is not arrived at like a traditional intention. The QE Intention itself is a singular thing, uncomplicated and straightforward. If you want a new house, you don't have to build it stick by stick or picture it vividly in your imagination. All you need is what is already waiting for you in your mind: your desire, the impression of your house that has already been formed. The desire for it was there even before you became aware of it. QE Intention is becoming aware of that already-created desire in a special way so that the forces of creation want you to have it. QE Intention properly positions your desire so that it becomes a part of and supports a greater plan.

All your desires remain with you on some level until they are fulfilled. Most of the time you will find them patiently settled in the quieter levels of your mind waiting to be acknowledged. So how do you acknowledge your desire-intention? Just become aware of it! But remember, the success of your intention depends on the quality of your awareness. Pure Eufeeling is the most refined experience of awareness we can have. When you become aware of your desire-intention while aware of Pure Eufeeling, it has the greatest potential for fulfillment on every level of your life.

When you do QE Intention, you form a partnership, as it were, with pure awareness. Pure awareness is the foundation for all creation. As pure awareness is projected through Eufeeling, it creates what you recognize as your life. Eufeeling, the purest expression of pure awareness, knows what it's doing. It is best to let it build your house for you. QE Intention deftly and delicately places your desire-intention in the most subtle expression of Eufeeling at the very seat of creation.

Do Nothing—Gain Everything

The ideal house for you may not be the one you have in your mind. Most of the time, an innocent desire from the very quiet level of your mind gets pushed about by your more bullish, less orderly thoughts. Eufeeling knows what is right for you better than you do, and it knows how to give it to you in the most efficient way without creating disharmony to yourself or others. If the house you have in your mind is right for you, then you will get it exactly as you see it. More than likely though, there is a much better house for you than you have imagined. Your nonspecific intention will give Eufeeling free reign to rally all the forces of creation around finding your perfect domicile.

The more specific you are, and the more willpower you impose on your intention, the more you distort the innocence of your original desire and the less likely you are to fulfill that desire. You may work very hard and get your house exactly as you see it in your mind but still not feel completely satisfied. Maybe you know someone who got exactly what they planned but couldn't enjoy it because it wasn't what they needed. So during the QE Intention process, when I ask you to become aware of your intention, just have a faint and easy idea of what you want. Then let Eufeeling do all the heavy lifting. Okay, ready to do nothing and get everything?

First become aware of what you want. Allow your thoughts to shift to the desire-intention that your mind has already created. Don't try to change it into something else; it is already perfect. Your desire has been created from you. In all creation there is not another like it. Acknowledge your desire, and accept it just as it is. Trying to make it into something better or more tangible will only change it into something less perfect. So when I ask you to think of your intention, all you have to do is become aware of what is already there. Simple enough, yes?

How to Have a QE Intention

Find a comfortable place to sit where you won't be disturbed for about 15 minutes. Settle in and begin the Quantum Entrainment process just as you learned earlier, but remain seated with your eyes closed. Start by watching your thoughts without effort or expectation. Soon, as before, your thoughts will slow down and become quieter or disappear altogether. Anywhere along the way, you may become aware of Eufeeling— a feeling of quietness, lightness, gentleness, peace, or some other good feeling. Because of your practice, you may find Eufeeling waiting for you as soon as you close your eyes. Wherever you find Eufeeling, allow your awareness to clearly and gently be with it. Allow the impulse of awareness to easily embrace the tender reflection of Eufeeling.

Continue your awareness of Eufeeling in this easy way for a full five minutes, or if you feel very quiet or still in mind and body, or if you have periods where you are unaware of your mind and body. (Be careful not to look ahead or anticipate these changes in body and mind. The increased mental activity of looking for them can keep them from occurring. The proper approach here is to just check to see if you have been unaware of body and mind or are feeling very quiet or still.)

Become aware of your Eufeeling. Identify it. Is it peace or a feeling of expansion, lightness, bliss, or joy? Just easily pay attention to what it is. Watch it like a cat watching a mouse hole, with eager attention to see what it will do next.

As you watch your Eufeeling in this quiet state, note that you feel some stillness. Now become more clearly aware of this stillness and observe it with quiet attention. You may be aware of stillness in your body as well. It is everywhere. Now note that while observing stillness, nothing is moving, including your mind. Everything is still, not moving. This is Pure Eufeeling. You know you are aware, but there is nothing to be aware of. Your body, your mind, all of creation is still as if holding its breath.

Now you are ready to gently create your QE Intention. Settled deeply within the stillness of Pure Eufeeling, let your mind easily shift over to your desire or intention. However it manifests in your mind, become aware of what it is that you want. This is just a flicker of a thought without any detail whatsoever. Actually, your intention is like a fine mist silently moving over the still surface of Pure Eufeeling, very delicate, very precious. Don't try to build or create an intention. Don't try to do anything. Only observe it in its most simple but complete state, innocent and pure. Quietly maintain your role solely as observer.

As you observe your intention, it may take on a life of its own. Thoughts may build around it, and a picture or story may <u>spontaneously</u> unfold. This is just right. Let that delicate mental activity unfold in whatever way it wants with you only observing. Let the picture/story unfold for no more than a minute or so.

Next let your awareness return to the stillness of Pure Eufeeling. If Pure Eufeeling is not there, then some aspect of Eufeeling (peace, joy, lightness, love) will be. Within that good feeling, you will always find stillness, as it is in everything. Observe the stillness as before until all movement stops. When you are once again aware of Pure Eufeeling, you have completed your QE Intention.

You can repeat this as many times as you like in each session. Follow each perception of stillness with an easy awareness of your desire-intention, and then return to stillness.

That is all there is to QE Intention. If your desire is motivated by a negative emotion like anxiety or guilt, you will find that you are already feeling better. That is the first of the fixing. But you have also started the wheels of creation in motion to bring you fulfillment on the material level. Now just sit back and watch as the genius of life opens opportunity after opportunity for you to enjoy.

Now let's go back and take a closer look at the actual mechanics of your QE Intention. The first element of QE Intention I want to pay particular attention to is Pure Eufeeling. It is the subtlest and most powerful awareness and therefore the most abstract. While QE Intention works best from awareness of Pure Eufeeling, it also works extremely well when you are aware of the less abstract feelings that are associated with Eufeeling. By that I mean the quietness, lightness, peace, joy, or bliss you feel when you are aware of Eufeeling. (Don't forget that the feelings of love and peace of Eufeeling come out of the stillness of Pure Eufeeling. They are the first activity in your mind after the non-activity of Pure Eufeeling.)

Here's my point. When you first begin doing QE Intention, you may not quite distinguish between the stillness of Pure Eufeeling and the peace or love of the more common Eufeeling. In fact, if you are searching for it, you may miss it. Searching is an activity and directly opposite to the innocent and simple observation of the non-activity of stillness. I know, I know . . . it's peculiar, but I didn't make the rules; I'm just here to point them out for you. The good news is that QE Intention works with either Eufeeling or Pure Eufeeling. I taught you QE Intention from the most refined perspective of Pure Eufeeling so you know that it exists. But you can just as easily, and with almost the same results, have a QE Intention by becoming aware of whichever feeling Eufeeling is generating in your mind. So your QE Intention might go something like this:

- Become easily aware of your Eufeeling (joy, peace, lightness), and then become aware of the stillness within the joy, peace, and lightness. The stillness is Pure Eufeeling. Easily let your awareness fall on the delicate form of your desire-intention, and quietly watch to see what happens.

- Gently return to the stillness of Pure Eufeeling after a few seconds, up to a minute or so.

For the sake of ease and to eliminate confusion, from this point on I will use the word *Eufeeling* to stand for both Pure Eufeeling and Eufeeling (with feeling). Then you will know that Pure Eufeeling is included every time I just use the word *Eufeeling*. However, in your practice of QE Intention, you will continue to look for Pure Eufeeling. Deal? Good, let's move on.

Let us spend a minute or two on intention. The QE Intention includes both the desire and the intention to fulfill that desire. When having a QE Intention, you can be consciously aware of both the desire and the intention, or you may find your awareness just falling on one without the other. While doing your QE Intention, you may only become aware of your desire or only your intention. In actuality, they come from a single source, and awareness of either one will satisfy both. Either is just right as long as you don't try to manipulate what reflects on the screen of your mind. Just have the impulse to become aware of your intention, and then whatever appears is just right. Again for the sake of simplicity, from now on I will just use the word *intention* to mean both the desire and the intention that goes hand in hand with it.

Of Puppies and Dandelion Puffs

Here's a simple way to have a QE Intention and have fun doing it. It has its own charm and is inherently as powerful as what I have previously described. I prefer this alternative method myself and use it almost exclusively. Here's how it goes.

After I have become aware of Eufeeling and have just become aware of my desire, I have a delicate thought that depicts the fulfillment of my desire in a fun and uplifting way. For instance, if my desire were to have a happier relationship with another person, I might have the thought *happiness of children at play* or *flowing as effortlessly as a river.* Then I let my mind return to Eufeeling, which will know exactly what to do with your QE Intention form. Don't make the thought into a story. Just a simple word or phrase is all you need. After all, it gave you the image to begin with. Now that you are conscious of your intention image, Eufeeling will put the wheels of creation in motion.

Many people prefer this method as it tends to add an element of lightness and play mirroring more closely the actual joy of creation. You can use any word or phrase that comes to your mind as long as it reflects the spirit of your intention. Just keep your intention image to a single word or short phrase, and have it show action. I'll give you some examples of forming intentions I have used. While you can use my intentions, it's better to eventually allow your own to surface in your consciousness. And keep in mind, these intentions can change between QE Intention sessions or even during them. Don't be rigid. Whatever pops into your mind and supports the fulfillment of your desire is just perfect. Here are a few of my examples:

Relationships

- Compassion of a mother
- Friendly as a dog
- Open like the sky
- Mysterious as the ocean

Finances

- Love as money
- Watering my money tree
- Giving from a bottomless well
- Money from my fingertips

Health

- Solid as a mountain
- Light as dandelion fuzz
- Clear as morning sunlight
- Flowing like the wind

Spiritual

- Still as a stone
- Knowing without knowing
- All things are my essence (Eufeeling)
- Light without flame

Making an Intention Sandwich

At times you may find your intention changing. If so, let it change the way it wants. It may seem to be going in a different direction than what you consciously want, but *don't interfere.* Let your intention express itself. What is happening at this point is that inner Self is reinventing the outer you. This is the rearrangement of the iron filings as the magnet (Eufeeling) lines up the chaotic elements of your life into perfect order. At this point you are open to all possible solutions from every direction of creation. This is not the case when you have an intention in common consciousness where control and imagination are not completely pure but subservient to either distorting emotions, fallible logic, or both.

You see, you have your intention lovingly nestled between slices of Eufeeling. You are creating something very special here. You could look at it as if you were making an intention sandwich. If Eufeeling were the bread, then you would be laying one slice on the table of pure awareness. On that still slice of Eufeeling bread, you lovingly place your intention meat (or soy burger for our vegan readers). Then place another slice of Eufeeling bread over your intention, and voilà . . . the perfect intention sandwich! Of course, I'm having a little fun with you, but this illustration makes the point that QE Intention is made in this way: Eufeeling-intention-Eufeeling.

Another way of looking at QE Intention is through the eyes of universal love. Universal love is like your mother. She wants you to have everything you desire. She doesn't see your desire as something separate from you, and she loves your desire as she loves you. When you have a QE Intention, universal love embraces it in her Eufeeling arms. She nurtures it, loves it, and encourages it to grow and prosper. If like a child you desire something that is harmful or wasteful, she will lead you in a different, more productive direction. She might even distract you with a greater gift that will quell your original desire and leave you with much, much more.

When you have a QE Intention and you gently lay your intention on the silent bed of Eufeeling, it can do one of two things. It may immediately fade away back into Eufeeling, or it may begin to take on a life of its own, like a movie. If so, watch as your intention movie plays on the screen of your awareness for a minute or so. Then allow your awareness to easily shift back to Eufeeling. If instead of a mental movie, your intention dissolved back into Eufeeling right away, then after a minute or so of stillness awareness, have the impulse to return to your intention.

So your intention either dissolves back into Eufeeling or some gentle thoughts unfold in your mind like a silent movie. Either experience is perfect. In either case, when you again become aware of Eufeeling, make sure you become very clearly aware of it. In that stillness watch Eufeeling carefully to see what will happen. After a minute or so with Eufeeling, again easily become aware of your intention. Continue this process alternating between Eufeeling and your intention. Gently repeat the cycle as many times as you like and as feels comfortable. This is how to have a QE Intention. Now finish the QE Intention session with two to five minutes, or longer if you like, of Quantum Entrainment—that is, being aware of Eufeeling whenever it is there and letting everything else go its separate way.

In essence, you are ever so delicately becoming aware of your intention and then letting the gentle and wise winds of Eufeeling blow it like mist into the silent reaches of your mind. You do not want to hold on to your intention in any way. Only let the impulse of your intention slip into your awareness, recognize it, and then let it dissolve back into the fullness of Eufeeling.

As I mentioned, it may be that instead of dissolving back into Eufeeling your intention begins to unfold its hidden parts like the petals of a blossoming flower. This is an automatic unfolding, not something you initiate. Just watch it like a movie being played on the screen of your mind. Do not interfere with this unfolding in any way. The universal creative forces are reorganizing time and events in your favor. This is how your life story gets rewritten. Your intention-movie may or may not make sense to you as it unfolds before you. No matter what plays out at this time, do not get involved. Only observe and enjoy. If you get wrapped up in your intention-movie and forget to return to Eufeeling for a couple of minutes, no problem. Just quietly return to Eufeeling when that sequence of thoughts fades out. On a similar note, your mind may begin to wander to unrelated topics. No problem here either. When you realize your mind is meandering, have a quiet impulse to return to pure Eufeeling and create another intention sandwich.

Many times while having a QE Intention, desires related to other parts of your life might show up. With QE Intention, you can kill two or three or more birds with one stone. All your desires are related to each other and all of them spring from the ego's basic desire to be reunited with Eufeeling. If other desires present themselves to you during a QE Intention session, it's okay to enjoy them as a substitute for your original intention. When you start a brand-new QE Intention session, however, always start with your original intention.

At times of great emotional stress, you may find that your QE Intention session is filled with thoughts. This might be less enjoyable than at other times, but many thoughts are not a problem. Don't fight the thoughts, thinking that you shouldn't be having them. If they're there, then that's exactly what you should be having. When you realize your mind is off topic, just begin to watch the thoughts attentively without trying to interfere just like when you learned the QE process. During these sessions, you probably won't experience the deep stillness of Pure Eufeeling. That's just fine. When the relative periods of quiet present themselves, become aware of your intention, then Eufeeling to whatever degree is open to you. Each QE Intention session will be different. Don't try to make them the same or make them different; accept what is there just as it is.

QE Intention will work for you, no matter what your subjective experience. (Note: if you are experiencing strong emotional discord during your QE Intention session, then I suggest reading Experience 1: "Healing the Emotional Body" in Chapter 27.)

For the most astonishing results, have several QE Intention sessions a day. At first I recommend you have your sessions last between five and ten minutes each. Besides mobilizing the creative forces of creation to fulfill your desires, there are many other benefits to a QE Intention session. In a very short time, you'll be able to have a QE Intention between heartbeats, anywhere, anytime. But don't get in a hurry. This is not a goal to shoot for, but something that will unfold naturally in its own time.

You can have QE Intention for any kind of a desire. It doesn't always have to be serious or important. Do QE Intention all day long. Have a QE Intention for the most frivolous of desires like a hot-fudge sundae or a new pair of nose tweezers. Go ahead, have a ball . . . you've earned it.

In the next few chapters, while you and QE Intention become good buddies, I will help you realize the power of the process you've just learned. I would like to go into more detail on how to apply QE Intention with such concerns as chronic illness, financial concerns, emotional management, and solving problems. I will also add techniques on how to help others over the hurdles to realizing their deepest desires. Before going on to the next chapter, I would like you to do another full QE Intention session. Go ahead, put the book in your lap, and let one of your desires drift to the surface of your consciousness. Now gently become aware of your Eufeeling . . . your intention . . . Eufeeling . . . and enjoy a full, blissful QE Intention session.

(Note: Even if you're not experiencing any particular emotional discord in your life, I recommend reading the next chapter on emotional management because it contains basic instructions that can be applied to the remaining chapters.)

CHAPTER 21

QE Intention for Emotional Distress

I don't think we really have to build a case for positive emotional health. I don't know a single individual who is beyond the touch of emotional discord. Even the Dalai Lama says he gets angry from time to time. All of us wrestle with negative emotions, and we often become overwhelmed to the point that our lives are negatively impacted.

The problem with runaway emotions is that they trample all over our logical faculties. Emotions bend and distort our ability to think clearly and tangibly. Typically those who are swayed by negative emotions aren't even aware that they have a problem; and when approached by well-meaning friends who point out their emotional aberrancy, the afflicted may look at them as if they just beamed down from a planet devoid of intelligent life. They simply can't believe that they have a problem, much less are the problem.

You can have a QE Intention for yourself or another person's welfare and feel completely confident that only good will be done. No, you don't need an individual's permission to have a QE Intention for him or her. That is because you are not doing anything. As you already know, once you have a QE Intention, you are done. Your intention is nestled in the nurturing arms of Eufeeling and will be worked out through Eufeeling's design, not yours.

Now I think this is obvious, but it needs to be said: I'm not trained in the psychological arts, and I don't feel that QE or QE Intention should be substituted for professional psychological care. QE and QE Intention are being used by professionals in the field of clinical psychology to help their patients overcome acute psychological trauma, as well as long-standing chronic concerns. Many of these professionals are excited to find that these Eufeeling technologies rapidly reduce the suffering of their patients. It is my hope that in the near future, we will be able to sponsor clinical studies as to the efficacy of QE in the field of psychology. In the meantime, know that for the layperson, QE and QE Intention is extremely valuable in reducing and eliminating psychological discord, but should never be substituted for the care of a licensed professional. Of course, this statement applies to all physical concerns in every field of health care. Now let's return to our regularly scheduled programming.

We have already talked about how an intention has two parts to it: the object and the emotion that gets attached to that object.

I separated intention into two parts mostly for the sake of illustration. You don't have to be concerned with these two aspects of intention unless you want to. QE Intention takes care of the whole ball of wax at one time without your having to do anything. That said, many people like to play with the parts of their intention while they are wrapped in the blanket of bliss we know as Eufeeling. This is completely a matter of preference. As long as you are aware of Eufeeling, your intention will be fulfilled as fully as the laws of nature will allow.

QE Intention for Emotions

(Note: I recommend that for the first several sessions of emotional QE Intention, you work with problems of a minor to moderate intensity. Once you feel comfortable and gain a little experience with the QE Intention process, then you can move on to more demanding emotional concerns.)

Sit quietly where you will not be disturbed for five to ten minutes. With eyes closed, allow your mind to become aware of what is bothering you. Bring up the situation and the emotions that go with it. Let it get as strong as it will, and then grade it on a scale from zero to ten, with ten being absolutely unbearable and zero being free of discomfort. Remember your starting number, as you will repeat this test when you're done with the session.

Do QE for two to three minutes and become aware of Eufeeling. You should feel some quietness in your mind and relaxation in your body. Let your mind go to the problem and then right away to how you would like to resolve the problem. These two steps, becoming aware of the problem and then the solution, is a fairly fluid process. You think of one then the other, and then let them both go as your awareness returns to Eufeeling. (Remember Eufeeling means the nothing of Pure Eufeeling or the feelings of simple Eufeeling. Either is fine.) Let's say that your mother-in-law was visiting, for example, and the two of you weren't getting along. This is how you could resolve the situation: From the easy fullness of Eufeeling, your mind becomes aware of the emotions you experience with your mother-in-law and the situation you have surrounding these emotions. You don't have to direct your mind in any way because you will find it drawn to the most troubling aspect all on its own. You only spend enough time on the emotions and situation to recognize it. That will happen in the time it takes you to have one or two thoughts. Then just as easily let your awareness go to the solution. Again, this is an automatic process so give your mind free reign. At this point, you might see your mother-in-law picking up her bags, giving you a great big hug, and boarding the plane to Seattle to take up residence in your sister-in-law's house. Your solution almost always presents itself without any conscious effort on your part. If it's a little stubborn, then you can prime the process by lightly thinking of a solution and letting that settle into Eufeeling. QE Intention is always fun and uplifting. Don't make it a chore, even when the subject matter is quite serious. Remember, you don't have to build your house stick by stick. Just a gentle nudge is all Eufeeling needs.

Have your QE Intention every minute or so for three to five minutes, and end your session with three to five minutes of Quantum Entrainment or just being aware of Eufeeling. Make sure you don't jump right up and launch yourself into activity. Allow your mind to wander for a while while you prepare for the day that awaits you. While you are taking this time, revisit the emotions and situation just as you did at the start of your QE Intention session. Let the emotions *get as strong as they will, and again, grade them on the zero-to-ten scale. In almost every case, you will find that your emotions—anxiety, fear, anger, sorrow, grief, guilt, or frustration—have dropped remarkably.*

Now, and this is very important, forget about what you've just done and go about your daily routine as if nothing has happened. Although a great deal has already occurred, most of it is going on behind the scenes. Leave it there. Let the organizing forces of creation do their job while you go about the businesses of living just as you always have. Believe me, your life will change immeasurably by what you have just done, or actually have just *not* done.

If you keep checking your life to see if your intention is working, you can actually hinder the process to a slight degree. Each time you check to see if progress has been made, you slightly recalibrate your intention from your present level of common consciousness. While you can never completely overshadow a single session of QE Intention, you can slow it down a bit. Fortunately, any distortions you might introduce will be neutralized by your next QE Intention session. So do your QE Intention session, and go about your life as usual. When your gift arrives, you will be surprised—not to mention grateful—and just a little awestruck. You did it without doing anything. It doesn't get any better than that.

Mist on the Water

In some systems of intention work and energy healing as well, creating waves of harmony is likened to dropping a pebble in a quiet pond. The traditional intention drops into the pond as waves move outward in concentric circles. The energy waves then return to you, the point at which the pebble disturbed the pond, bringing with them information on how to be successful in your world. Having a QE Intention is more like allowing an ethereal mist to settle ever so lightly on the still waters of Pure Eufeeling.

We do not want to disturb those waters, but allow them to remain a clear reflection of creation. We do not want to endeavor to impose our limited will on creation. Even to think so is folly and only fosters the illusion of control, which quickly leads to stronger desires and ultimately increased suffering. Rather, from our silent vantage point on the surface of the still pond of Pure Eufeeling, we tenderly open our awareness to our QE Intention then watch as it softly kisses the surface of Pure Eufeeling.

This is the magical moment, the flawless conception when all of creation awakens to your desire. Your work is done. On the most precious level of life, your desire has already been fulfilled. Your disruptive desires and unsettling emotions have dissipated like a cool mist in warm sunlight. Now with a sense of playful expectancy, you need only wait to see in what wrapping your present will arrive.

CHAPTER 22

Helping Others with Chronic Illness

Chronic illnesses are long lasting, involve prolonged care, and have a fairly low cure-rate percentage. As our bodies and minds age, our ability to spontaneously repair damaged tissues diminishes. Old age sees a greater share of chronic illnesses, and a lower percentage of these cases are cured. Although chronic illnesses are certainly not restricted to our older population, that is where you will find a plethora of these conditions, including arthritis, heart disease, diabetes, and, the most commonly feared, cancer. The death rate from chronic illnesses is high even among younger sufferers. Chronic illness creates a sizable burden on family members, the community, and even entire countries. Obviously, the greatest burden is carried by the individual who has such a disease, and it is the individual sufferer who will benefit most from QE Intention.

If you don't have a chronic illness but would like to help someone who does, then QE Intention is tailor-made for you. Here's how to go about helping a chronically suffering friend, family member, or even a perfect stranger by having a QE Intention.

QE Intention for Helping Others with Chronic Illness

Do Quantum Entrainment for three to five minutes or until you feel quite settled in Eufeeling. Become aware of the individual (your partner) and how the illness is affecting her. Do this as if you were watching her from across the room, as a simple observer of her outward condition. If you begin to feel a little emotional, don't worry. Your personal involvement will not diminish the effectiveness of your QE Intention, and it will also be considerably healing for you. Don't try to feel the emotion or push it out. If you become emotionally involved, acknowledge that you are and continue with your awareness of your partner's symptoms. You only need to spend from a few seconds to 10 or 15 seconds, and then let everything dissolve into Eufeeling. Remember to become clearly and attentively aware of it. Enjoy the easy feeling of Eufeeling for a minute or so.

Now have a simple thought of your partner. Picture her as before with the symptoms; and this time, become aware that her body, mind, and emotions are filled with the bliss of Eufeeling. Recognize that her every thought and emotion is submerged in the beauty of Eufeeling. Acknowledge that every atom of every molecule of every cell in your partner's body is alive with the harmony and healing influence of Eufeeling. Innocently observe your mental movie to see how she reacts. Do this for a minute or so, and then return to Eufeeling. Repeat this three-phase process one or two more times, observing symptoms, becoming aware of Eufeeling, watching how your partner responds to being filled with Eufeeling, and finally back to Eufeeling. Finish your QE Intention session with three to five minutes of Quantum Entrainment.

The power and speed at which QE Intention works for chronic sufferers is nothing short of amazing. QE Intention always has an immediate effect. How quickly you will see results in symptomatology depends on the type and severity of illness and the sufferer's constitution. If you're able to get objective feedback, such as blood-sugar and blood-pressure readings, you will see improvement right away. Also consider having your partner do the pre- and post-test for both physical and emotional discomfort. Again, in most cases you will see immediate, and many times drastic, results.

Stick precisely to the simple formula described above. Ego plays no part in QE Intention, so we should not envision our partners as healing or as being healed. This will not help in the recovery. We are not the healer; QE Intention is not the healer. Healing will come from the creative forces that issue forth from the wisdom and compassion inherent in Eufeeling. Whether our partners are cured or not is really not up to us. We can have the desire and the intention for our partner to heal, and this is as it should be. But the infinite number of possibilities in which the disease process can be expressed is beyond the comprehension of our limited minds. Better we respect the unfolding of the forces of nature as beyond our control.

Do QE Intention, and then enjoy being present with your partner or just go on with your business as usual. When it's time, Mother Nature will tap you on the shoulder and let you have a look at her handy work.

You Can't Manufacture Nonattachment

Having a QE Intention for a chronic illness that is manifesting in your body-mind needs a slightly different orientation than when you do this work for someone else. As you might suspect, when you work on yourself you have a vested interest in the outcome and therefore tend to be more attached to the results. This attachment is fear motivated and filtered through your ego. Consequently, effectiveness is diminished significantly. So the trick with self–QE Intention is nonattachment.

You cannot manufacture nonattachment. You cannot try to be unattached to your illness or anything else for that matter. Trying means effort toward a goal; a goal means that there is a path involved. It says that where you are is not good enough and you want to be somewhere better. You want to change what is. If life is perfect just as it is, then wanting to change it means that you deny the perception of present perfection.

I can just hear you thinking with some measure of incredulity, *Of course I don't want to be where I am. I'm chronically ill! I want to be free of my illness.* This is obvious when you are ill. Where you are is not where you want to be, and you strive to reach your goal of being free of your disease . . . but that is just the point I want to make. It is a subtle and therefore potent shift in perception that can make all the difference between living life in fullness or in suffering, regardless of whether or not you have a life-threatening disease.

When you have a chronic illness, the main issue is not really the disease but your perception of it. If you own your body and your mind, when it's threatened in any way, your very essence is threatened. Ego thinks the body-mind is his, and he spends huge amounts of energy trying to protect it. Ego feels that if the body-mind dies, it too will die. QE Awareness transcends ego awareness and knows that destruction of the body-mind does not lead to destruction of Self. As we've already discussed, the essence of Self is timeless and beyond destruction.

I don't mean to sound offhanded, but bodies come and go. It is often said by those who have suffered deeply that there are worse things than death. The worst thing you can do to life is attach to death. As soon as your body is born, it begins dying. Attachment to your body is attachment to death. No matter how hard ego tries to keep things together, in the end your temple will collapse. There are a lot of things that illness can teach you, but ultimately there is only one lesson worth learning: You are not your body-mind. You are unbounded grace and joy and love all wrapped up in the celestial shell of Eufeeling. What good is it to beat a disease but lose your soul in the process? One thing is guaranteed: as you age, illness and infirmity will follow. Yes, you can cheat death a little here and there, but in the end, the house always wins.

Neither denying the fear nor attacking it will work to give us the inner peace we so desperately seek. For that we already have everything we need. When we have a QE Intention, we forfeit the field of death in favor of the joy of living beyond bounds.

CHAPTER 23

Your Chronic Illness: The QE Emotion Body Scan

Start by sitting comfortably with your eyes closed, and do Quantum Entrainment for three to five minutes or until the quiet stillness of Eufeeling is with you. Now become aware of any discomfort or symptoms that you have, even if you do not attribute them to your illness. Let your awareness easily scan your body. As you become aware of each indication of illness in your body, let your awareness linger there for a few seconds before moving to the next symptom. When you've finished scanning your body in this way (and this should take no more than a minute or two), have the impulse to return to Eufeeling.

After a minute or so of being aware of Eufeeling, have the thought to return to your body. Again, pay attention to the different regions of your body and the symptoms that appear there. Note that these symptoms may have moved or may have increased or decreased in intensity, or you may even become aware of new symptoms that did not appear the first time. This is an indication that healing is already taking place. Regardless of what or where the symptom is, when you become aware of it, this time look to see if there is an emotion attached to that symptom. If you find an emotion attached to the symptom, just easily observe it for several seconds and then move on to the next symptom. Both the body scan and the emotional scan should last no more than a minute or two each. Now return to the stillness and peace of Eufeeling for about a minute.

Again easily allow your awareness to fall on your body-mind, including the attached emotions. Become aware of your body, your symptoms, and your emotions at the same time you are aware of Eufeeling. Recognize that every thought, sensation, and emotion is submerged in Eufeeling. Your symptom and emotion are there at the same time Eufeeling is there. Notice that every atom of every molecule of every cell in your body is alive with the harmony and healing influence of Eufeeling. Give it no direction. Resist the urge to direct energy to a specific area of illness or discomfort. This will be done by Eufeeling far more effectively and quickly than by limited you. Enjoy doing nothing and being everything for a minute or two, and return to the welcoming arms of Eufeeling for a minute or so. Repeat this three-phase process three or more times, as you like. Remember to separate each phase—the body scan, the emotional scan, and the realization of Eufeeling—and all three simultaneously with a minute *or so of awareness of Pure Eufeeling. Finish your QE Intention session with three to five minutes of Quantum Entrainment.*

If you are bedridden, you may want to rest for a longer period with your eyes closed or even take a nap. When you are ill, you can do QE and QE Intention just as often as you like. Although neither is a healing technique, the Eufeeling generates a huge and harmonious healing energy that will flood your body-mind, allowing it to heal much, much, more quickly.

You may have noticed that at no time during the QE Intention do you direct energy, nor do you imagine healing taking place or in any way interject control into the process. You are only encouraged to move your awareness from one perception of relative reality to another. So the only exertion involved in QE Intention is the almost effortless impulse to become aware. Herein lies the secret to the power and remarkable effectiveness of QE Intention.

CHAPTER 24

QE Intention for Wealth and Prosperity

When you sit down and think about it, we humans need very little to survive and not much more to make life comfortable. But how much wealth does it take to make us happy? We can answer that question by asking, "How empty does your ego feel?" Our happiness depends on our relative state of affairs.

This year, for instance, you might be happy to ride a bike to a job you're lucky to have. After a few years of financial success, you might feel bored with your Mercedes. Happiness will always be dependent on relative circumstances, but the need to be happy has a single, constant cause. The spur to greater happiness springs from the ego's need to feel full, to reunite with Eufeeling. Striving for material wealth in common consciousness is the outward expression of the ego's inward search for completion. In QE Awareness one doesn't strive for wealth and one isn't dependent on it for happiness. Oddly enough, great wealth often comes to those who are living in accordance with the expression of Eufeeling.

Happiness Is Relative—Eufeeling Is Permanent

When we lose awareness of Eufeeling, we feel something is missing and it is. We become aware of Eufeeling and note that we have no fear, anxiety, guilt, or anger because Eufeeling is the ultimate goal of every thought and action we have. All suffering, feelings of emptiness, are filled when we have a clear awareness of Eufeeling. We can still feel sad or anxious, but we cannot suffer from those emotions if we are with Eufeeling. It's just not possible. But when we forget and drift away from Eufeeling, we feel the loss and try to fill it with things and philosophies and relationships. It will never work.

The "mistake of the ego" is that gathering those things into itself will eventually remove the empty feeling. It wants to swim on the surface of life, owning all that it surveys. It won't work—it can't. What ego needs to do is stop swimming. If it does, it thinks it will sink to the depths of the ocean of mind and cease to exist. Ego feels that if it stops trying to amass wealth in any of its various and wonderful forms, it can never be full . . . but nothing could be further from the truth. When it does stop trying, it will in actuality be granted the greatest gift of all. When ego stops trying to survive is when it opens itself to the fullness of life.

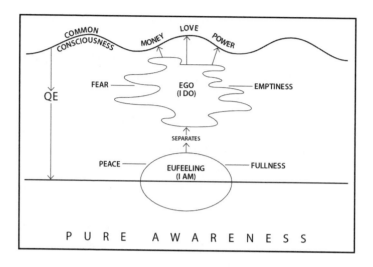

Those living in QE Awareness who don't amass vast wealth don't need it. That said, there is colossal abundance in this world, and it sure is fun to share in it. There is always a sense of gratitude and awe when we receive a gift given through Eufeeling. One feels that there is a playful impishness working behind the scenes. You don't have the feeling that you earned the gift but that it was given to you for the sheer joy of the giving. Aware of the infinite love of the giver, you are unattached to the gift and can just as easily pass it on to another as keep it for yourself.

The first rule to amass inner or outer wealth is: *Before all else, have awareness of Eufeeling.* Once you have taken this first step, you have acquired the greatest treasure a human can know: Self-awareness. Settled in the seat of Self, all actions you perform honor and support your Self. From then on the world is your playground. Having a QE Intention for abundance removes the fear, anxiety, and sense of desperation many have when they deeply desire something. Having a QE Intention is fun. It is accomplished with a sense of playful detachment.

When you have a QE Intention for greater wealth, you will work on two levels: quelling of the emotions attached to the desire, and manifestation of the material condition. The emotions that are attached to the object or situation will immediately dissolve into absolute quiescence. There are a wide variety of emotional sharks swimming around a financial concern. You might recognize them as anxiety or fear, frustration, anger, and confusion. Minutes after having a QE Intention, these emotions along with their negative influence, will significantly abate or disappear altogether. Free of this emotional bullying, you can sit back and wait for your desire to be fulfilled.

QE Intention for Material Wealth

Find a comfortable chair where you will not be disturbed for five to ten minutes. Close your eyes, and do the Quantum Entrainment process for three to five minutes or until you feel the quiet presence of Eufeeling. Let your mind go to your desire for greater wealth. For five to ten seconds, watch what your mind shows you about what you want, the fulfillment of that desire. If you have negative emotions attached to your desire for greater wealth, identify them. Let them grow strong and vivid in your mind, and when they are as strong as they can be, grade them on the zero-to-ten scale, with ten being unbearable.

Easily allow your mind to return to Eufeeling for a minute or so. After a minute has pasted, have the impulse to return to your desire for greater wealth. For

*the next minute or so, let your mind play the movie
about what you want. Your mind may automatically
show you a movie of what it is like to have actually
achieved your desire. If so, watch the movie, making
sure that you don't interfere with the plot. Eufeeling
is reorganizing and removing the impediments to the
full realization of your desire. After a minute or two,
return to Eufeeling.*

*Repeat the process of revisiting your desire three
to five times, making sure to separate each episode
with awareness of Eufeeling. If you had negative emotions and did the pretest before your QE Intention session, now is the time to do your posttest. Do exactly
as you did at the beginning of the session, and note
the strength of your emotions on the scale. Even in the
most desperate cases, you will see significant and immediate dissipation of negative emotions. Many times
negative emotions surrounding financial concerns
are more damaging than the actual situation itself. If
all you were able to do was eliminate these draining
emotions from your financial concerns, that would be
worth the price of this book alone. Make sure to take
enough time to transition from your quiet state to a
state of greater activity by opening and closing your
eyes and stretching before you get out of the chair.*

Life Is an Easter-Egg Hunt

What must you do now to realize your desire of greater
wealth? Absolutely nothing! This is perhaps the hardest
part for the mind controlled by common consciousness. It
will feel that there's a need to do something to make it all

work out. If you find this to be the case, do QE and take your common conscious mind to QE Awareness. You will not feel the need to do or to keep checking to see if things are working out. You will have infinite patience, and your patience will be rewarded.

All the organization is being taken care of on the finest and most powerful level of creation. Not much you can do to help out there. However, that does not mean that you sit on your thumbs. At this point you need to be open to opportunities when they present themselves. Stir the pot a little. Think of it like an Easter-egg hunt where Mother Nature has hidden an infinite number of eggs for you to find. Each represents the complete fulfillment of your desire, so you only have to find one. Look at every interaction, person, or situation in your life as a bush or a rock that may be hiding your Easter egg. Look for your treasure with a sense of ease and playfulness. Meanwhile, make sure that you continue to have a QE Intention session two or three times a day. Happy hunting!

CHAPTER 25

Helping Others Find Material Wealth

The best way to get is to give. Even if you're wallowing in poverty, you will find immediate inspiration when you have a QE Intention to help someone else find material wealth. Here's how to do it:

Find a comfortable chair where you will not be disturbed for five to ten minutes. Close your eyes, and do the Quantum Entrainment process for three to five minutes or until you feel the quiet presence of Eufeeling. Let your mind go to your partner, the person you want to help. For five to ten seconds, entertain quiet thoughts about how you interpret his or her problem. If the individual is suffering, identify the negative emotions as you see them. Easily shift your awareness from your thoughts about them to Eufeeling. Enjoy the fullness of Eufeeling for a minute or so, and then let your thoughts return to your partner.

As your mental movie plays, observe your partner to see if she becomes more acutely aware of her emotions and physical posture. No matter how she reacts, as you observe quietly and attentively, also become aware of Eufeeling. Then like a cat watching a mouse hole, continue to be aware of her body and emotions and Eufeeling. The stillness or piece or bliss that you are feeling is also alive in your partner. Observe Eufeeling in your partner for a minute or so, and return to the perception of Eufeeling within yourself.

Alternate between your perception of your partner and Eufeeling three to five times before ending your QE Intention session. There is no need for you to see your partners attaining their desire. When you do QE Intention for someone else, greater material affluence is implied. You are providing the foundation upon which that will happen, but how that happens is not really your concern. You will find great inner satisfaction when doing QE Intention for others' material wealth, and your own efforts to improve your prosperity will also be enhanced. So make it a habit to help out a friend or two every day. You will be absolutely delighted in your own rewards.

CHAPTER 26

Solving Problems with QE Intention

There are no problems in nature. Problems are a man-made phenomenon. They rise out of the human need to impose order on the environment. To the human mind, an orderly environment is one that can be controlled; this order is relative. The degree of disorder depends on the perspective of the observer, and the perspective of the observer depends on his or her perception of harmony. If you perceive your world as a collection of thoughts and things, some of which are related to each other and some are not, then you are languishing in the confusion of common consciousness. If on the other hand, you feel that everything is just right just as it is, then you are enjoying QE Awareness.

At its most basic level, Eufeeling only has one moving part. We can't get much more harmonious than that. One cannot be at odds with itself. It takes two to create that phenomenon. When Eufeeling splinters into the infinite shards of creation, the human mind cannot keep track of all that stuff doing all those things. Except in the most limited sense, cause and effect are beyond comprehension. We try, but we're just not capable of knowing everything. Here is where problems are born, or should I say the illusion of disharmony that we call a problem.

We can't possibly know the result that a single thought or action will have but still we try. This is where letting go comes in. I don't mean consciously saying something like, "Okay now, Frank, take a deep breath and just let go." You cannot consciously let go. Conscious effort is still effort, and you cannot make an effort to be effortless. What I'm talking about here is more of an acceptance of what is then a letting go. We cannot accept or believe that everything will be okay when we see that our actions consistently fall short of their mark. We can try to make ourselves believe that we are in control, but that is merely laying one illusion over another. One has to invest a great deal of time and energy into maintaining such a belief.

Acceptance comes naturally from knowing your unbounded, inner Self to be in control. This knowing is not an understanding but the deepest intuition that perfection permeates all form. This realization grows automatically out of the joy, bliss, and love that is you, that is Eufeeling. Any problem has at its roots the ego-oriented, fear-driven perception of the world through common consciousness. And guess what? You can't fix common consciousness with common consciousness. That's like replacing one broken part in a car engine with a different broken part. The engine may function differently, but it will still be broken. Fortunately, common consciousness is easily remedied. You already know how to do it: Quantum Entrainment.

So that takes care of the primal problem of problem solving, but how are we to go about solving specific mysteries, the puzzles that present themselves to us every day?

How do we find the time for a vacation when we've already used up all our vacation days? How do we get three kids to three different activities in three different parts of town at the same time? How do we end a relationship creating as little harm as possible?

Why, you already know how to do that as well: QE Intention . . . with a twist.

QE Intention and Problem Solving

Find a comfortable chair where you will not be disturbed for 10 to 15 minutes. Close your eyes, and do the Quantum Entrainment process for three to five minutes or until you feel the quiet fullness of Eufeeling. Now easily let your mind go to your problem, taking the time to review every aspect of it. Don't try to solve the problem. This is very important. Become the perfect observer of the problem as your mind presents it to you. Quietly observe any emotions associated with it, keeping alert disinterest as they diminish and disappear. Continue to let your mind wander over the various aspects of your problem. Do this for one to three minutes, and then easily become aware of Eufeeling.

After a minute or so with Eufeeling, return to pick up the mental threads of your problem movie. Let the thoughts about the problem unfold with you as the interested spectator. Don't be in a hurry, and don't look for a solution; just be acutely aware of the movie playing on the screen of your mind. Do this for one to three minutes, and then return to Eufeeling for a minute or so. Repeat this cycle three to five times. When finished, open your eyes and take time to ease yourself back into activity. Or if you have the time, remain sitting in your chair, and allow yourself to daydream as long as you feel comfortable to do so.

Traditionally, solutions will come when they are unlooked for. You might find that the answer comes to you just before falling asleep at night or is waiting for you when you wake up in the morning. It may also pop into your mind at any other time during the day, usually during times of reduced concentration like washing the dishes or driving your car. Give yourself plenty of space, and don't stress to find an answer. You can easily do several sessions of solving problems with QE Intention throughout the day. The best times are first thing in the morning and just before you go to bed at night, but any time will work just fine.

CHAPTER 27

Crafting the Perfect Relationship

Every time we perceive something, we have a relationship with it. It doesn't matter if it's a rock, a paper clip, another human being, or one of our thoughts. Even when we are self-absorbed, we are in a relationship with ourselves. Life is one continual relationship.

There are only two ways we can have a relationship: in common consciousness or in QE Awareness. I'm guessing that right around 99 percent of the world's population relates to themselves, to each other, and to their environment in common consciousness, unaware of their own basic inner essence. If people are unaware of their inner essence, they lose their orientation and have no reference point from which to view the world. They become top-heavy, leaning precariously toward the allurement of the outer life.

The inner self is the foundation upon which the outer self, the "me" is built. Because it is incomplete, a baseless perception always looks to gain something from relationships. For instance, when we perceive a rock, our mind will naturally look for a way to use it to our advantage. *Could I take it home to beautify my yard? Could I use it to open a walnut? I wonder if it's a good rock for skipping across water.*

If your mind perceives no use for the rock, it moves on to the next perceived thing. The feeling in your mind might be something like: *This rock is like so many others I've seen, and it offers no particular value. Since I'm looking for value in life, I'll move on to the next object.*

In terms of its general orientation, it's really no different to your mind whether it is interacting with a rock or a person. The common conscious mind always looks to gain something from a relationship. The common conscious mind needs constant stroking to feel alive. It is like a bottomless pit into which it keeps throwing everything it can get its hands on in an effort to fill it. But things and thoughts can never fill the emptiness for long. Here's what I mean.

Let's say that George and John work at the same company, and they bump into each other at the office coffee machine one morning during their break.

John says, "Hi, George. How's everything going?"

"Oh," George sniffles pathetically, "I'm catching a head cold."

"Well, that's nothing," John replies. "I've had a head cold and allergies for a week now."

"Oh yeah," George retorts, "My wife has walking pneumonia!"

"I'm sorry for your wife, George," John says unsympathetically, "but my wife has double pneumonia and has been confined to bed for a month."

And so it goes, each ego trying to coax from the other some sympathy, some sense of recognition and, lacking that, looks to dominate the other ego. Here John and George are looking to be recognized for their suffering. They could just as easily be talking about their accomplishments at work ("I just closed a big deal for the company!") or who they know ("The mayor's secretary and my wife go bowling together!").

Not too infrequently you'll find a variation on this theme, a kind of "reversed psychology" attempt at recognition in the form of insincere flattery. I remember two women talking at the gym. Agnes had obviously lost a lot of weight recently and opens the conversation with her friend by saying, "Are you losing weight, Susan?"

"Not really," Susan responds, somewhat puzzled until she takes a closer look at Agnes. "But I see that you've dropped a few pounds."

"Oh, really?" Agnes replies coyly. "I didn't think it showed. I have Raul coaching me—you know, he's the one who trains models. I've been buying only the best foods from Très Bon Epicurean Market, and I've been taking private tennis lessons from Steele Gray. He says I have talent! You know Steele—he's that young blond tennis instructor with the cute . . . "

And so it goes.

This is a loose translation of the actual conversation, and I have changed the names to protect the innocent, but you get the idea. Agnes gave away a compliment in order to receive one, and to boast about her recent acquirements and drop a few names in the process.

If you look around, you may become more aware of just how many people are practicing these forms of one-upmanship and "give a little to get a lot" relationships all in an effort to feel more whole. The thing is, these relationships only make us feel more hollow. When two people come together with the idea of only taking, both walk away ultimately unfulfilled. In common consciousness, it can be no other way.

But when two people have a conversation aware of Eufeeling, aware of the joy and fullness that they are, relationships take on a totally different dimension. They do not need another person to make them feel complete. They are already settled in the joy of being fully human. These people do not have to try to give. Giving becomes a natural, spontaneous outpouring of the stuff that we all desire. These people radiate the love of life, Eufeeling, and we all benefit.

Right now, I would like to examine more closely a relationship between human beings. More specifically, let's look at the relationship between two people who are in love, the romantic relationship. I think this is an excellent place to start for two reasons. First, almost all of us have fallen in love at one time in our life. Second, and more important, it can teach us the two fundamental experiences for developing a relationship built on the foundation of universal love.

You know romantic love. That's when your whole world turns upside down. You think about the other person every minute of every day. You don't sleep, but you have unbounded energy. When you are not together, time interminably drags on and on. When you are, time holds its breath and you will do anything to stay with the person, revolving around each other in a mutually generated eternity.

Your lover is perfection. He loves the way she scrunches up her little nose when she chews her food. She loves his masculine smell and the way he looks after his body. Your new love is beautiful and strong and kind and wise. You just can't get close enough to your beloved. You wish you could be inside of the person. You feel like you could just eat them up, they are so delicious.

This overwhelming, exuberant rush of romantic love can last for days! Okay, okay, it can last longer, sometimes months, but sooner or later romantic love has to end. And when it does, you are left in a different kind of daze. You may look at your love and wonder where all the excitement went. You may even wonder if they are the same person you fell in love with. They seem to take more energy and have less tolerance. They seem distant and disinterested and, well, they seem to easily get on your nerves. Now he can't stand her snuffling nose and the smacking noise she makes when she eats. She wishes that he would bathe more often and stop looking at his muscles in the mirror. Before she was so cute, he wanted to eat her up. Now he wishes he had. Romantic love is fleeting. No matter what we do to recapture it, we can never duplicate those first magnificent moments of apparent intimacy.

Why? Why can't we maintain the intensity of those early days? Because romantic love is conditional love, and we humans were built for a much grander adventure. Even the more mature love that builds between two people over a lifetime is largely dependent on conditions. In the beginning of such a relationship, we may feel we are honest and open with the other person. We feel that if we work together, we will grow in love together, but that is an illusion. It is as if you and your partner were standing on opposite rails of a train track that stretches out before you and disappears into the horizon. On the horizon the two rails appear to meet, to come together at a single point, but that is an illusion. No matter how far we travel together on our separate rails on the railroad of life (I know, I know . . . that's really corny), when we reach the horizon, we will still be separate. That's because we are human, and being human means being unique.

No two see the world in exactly the same way. We have different needs, interests, talents, life experiences, genes, physical needs, and so on. All of these characteristics affect how we see our world. Two people in a long-term relationship are especially aware of the differences between each other. In fact, it is the differences that complement our relationships. They strengthen them, give them energy and flexibility. But love is not built on differences; it grows out of that which is the same in us.

Like two flowers in a garden, each has its roots in the same fertile soil. Drawing nourishment from the soil, they radiate their innate and individual beauty to be enjoyed by the other. If they cannot draw sustenance from the soil, they weaken. In their weakness they neither reflect their full beauty nor can they appreciate the beauty of another.

It is this same soil that supports and feeds the two flowers. It is the unbounded nature and pure reflection of Eufeeling that supports and nourishes each of us. Eufeeling is that single soil, and when we are aware of Eufeeling, we are aware of that sameness from which we all draw our basic sustenance. Awareness of Eufeeling brings peace and joy and love. Awareness of Eufeeling in others does the same.

Unconditional love is unbounded love, meaning that it is everywhere all the time. You do not have to work together over a lifetime to become something that you already are. It is not hard to grow in unbounded love together; it is impossible! You already have all the love that you need—or more accurately, you already are the love that you seek. You need only become aware of it. So let's now look at the common conditional love relationship and see how we can add to it the element of infinity.

We will begin by examining an argument where you and your partner are angry with each other. First we will separate you so that we can calmly examine what anger is, how to neutralize it, and how to replace it with the perception of Eufeeling. You'll do this on your own, separate from your partner. You will find it a very gentle, nurturing, and uplifting experience. You do not have to fight with yourself to find peace. Once your perception of Eufeeling has been reestablished, then we will bring you and your partner back together for a healing conversation. This will not be the typical common consciousness conversation like the one noted earlier between John and George. This conversation will take place in QE Awareness, spreading a soothing salve over the open wounds that anger left days or even just moments before.

Now let's say that you and your partner are having an argument and are openly angry with each other. Let's look at what is happening in terms of activity—in this case, mental activity. More activity means less order. Order is a synonym for harmony and healing. So the more activity we experience in the mind, the less harmony and healing it will reflect. Conversely, the less activity we experience, the more peace and harmony will manifest. Awareness of pure awareness is awareness of nothing, which is total inactivity. Research on the four main levels of awareness—waking, dreaming, deep sleep, and pure awareness—show that when we are aware of pure awareness, we are receiving the deepest rest possible; deeper even than the rest we get in deep sleep. That's why Quantum Entrainment gives us so deep a healing in such a short time.

During QE Awareness we dip into pure awareness, then become aware of Eufeeling, which means we are thinking quietly and orderly. This would actually constitute a fifth main level of human awareness where we're not sitting still in pure awareness but actually performing our daily activities from a quiet, orderly level of mental activity. Living life from the level of QE Awareness means that we hurt less and heal more. When two people communicate with each other from the level of QE Awareness, they are mutually and completely supportive of each other. Neither needs to take from the other because they are already full of Eufeeling. Neither person need rely on the content of the conversation for personal recognition or other forms of self-satisfaction. Both could be in total bliss while talking about something as mundane as the weather. Both people enter into the conversation without the need to take from the other. Each sees their inner essence reflecting back to them through the eyes of their partner. Both give and receive what is needed and walk away fulfilled.

This is how you will craft the perfect relationship. In times of stress and upheaval, you simply allow any anger, guilt, frustration, anxiety, or fear to absolve in the nurturing waters of Eufeeling. Then from that quiet level of QE Awareness, you reconnect with your partner and share the joy of being fully human.

Let's say that you and your partner have become angry over some issue. Even though you may feel that your partner's position on the issue, or the issue itself, is the source of anger, it is not. It is the mind lost in common consciousness that looks for reasons outside itself as the source of anger. They are not. You might blame the heavy traffic, an inconsiderate co-worker, or an unsympathetic policeman for your ill temper. But that same situation at a different time or with a different person may not bother you at all.

Neither is anger the enemy. Emotions are part of life. We consider a person without them to be pathological. We just don't want emotions crashing over us, submerging the joys of our life beneath their roiling waters. At one time or another, all of us mortals are overwhelmed by a negative emotion. However, a destructive emotion is not the cause. It is the symptom.

Now let's return to the argument you're having with your partner. Remember that more activity means less order. When you are angry, your mind becomes more active and less orderly. You know this because during an argument, you may say stupid or hurtful things that you would never say when you are calm.

Did you ever end a particularly aggressive argument, and a short time later, the lightbulb goes on in your head and you think, *Oh, I should have said that! It really would have made my point.*

This is a perfect example of more orderly thinking coming out of a quieter mind. As soon as you walk away from an argument, your mind begins settling down and is able to think more logically. It is just this process that we will enlist to overcome the deleterious effects of anger, quickly opening awareness to the healing and harmony of Eufeeling.

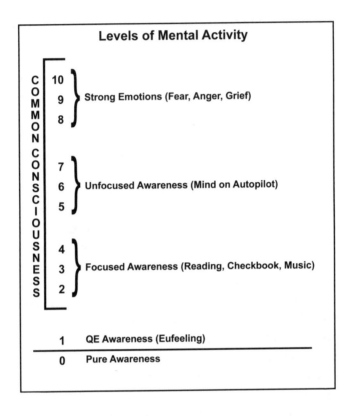

When you become aware of pure awareness, there is no activity in your mind. In this chart, the zero below the horizontal line represents the non-activity of pure awareness. The number one, above the horizontal line, indicates QE Awareness, awareness of Eufeeling. Numbers five through seven stand for the ordinary mental activity experienced when we are in common consciousness and our mind is on autopilot. This is where most people spend most of their time during the day. Numbers two through four represent more focused common conscious thinking, like when we balance our checkbook, attentively listen to a Mozart sonata, read a book, or plan a vacation. Finally, numbers eight through ten correspond to the more excited levels of mental activity we might experience during strong emotions like fear, anger, grief, and even the overwhelming exuberance we experience in the throes of romantic love.

Remember, in terms of activity, the more active your thinking, the less logical and the less active your mental activity; the less active your thinking, the more logical, harmonious, healing, and loving. So the first thing you want to do when you're having an argument with your partner (numbers eight through ten) is to separate yourself from the situation. As soon as you walk away, your anger will immediately begin to dissipate.

Continue this "cooling down" period until your mind reaches focused awareness (numbers two through four). It is in focused awareness that your mind will be free from anger's influence. (Note: if you are experiencing unfocused awareness [numbers five through seven], your mind is absorbed in its own activity beyond your conscious control.) Once you are experiencing focused awareness, you will be able to effortlessly do Quantum Entrainment. When you do QE, you will first experience the deeper rest of pure awareness (number zero) and then the healing effects of QE Awareness (number one). So how do you initiate this first step of moving from full-blown, eye-popping anger to focused awareness and then Eufeeling? I'm so glad you asked. . . .

If you are presently experiencing focused awareness, you can begin by sitting in a comfortable chair and closing your eyes. If you're besieged by anger, you may not immediately be able to sit down or close your eyes. You may find yourself pacing the floor and talking to yourself while you pound your fist into your hand. You will be replaying all the elements of the argument in your head. You will be swept away by the flood of the emotion, unable to sit down much less close your eyes. This is fine. Simply follow the directions below even if you are unable to sit down. Proceed in whatever position, or state of mind, you find yourself. When the time is right, take a seat, close your eyes, and continue in the sitting position.

Experience #1: Healing the Emotional Body

Sit comfortably in a chair, and close your eyes. Let your mind go back to the source of the anger. (This exercise can be used to heal any overpowering emotion, including fear, guilt, sadness, and so on.) Become aware of the person, the situation, and especially the anger that you felt. Replay the whole scene in your mind. Let your anger become as strong as you can. Now allow your awareness to switch to your body. Emotions always express themselves somewhere in your body. Become aware of your whole body at one time. Note the places where you feel physical uneasiness or tension due to the anger. This emotion can affect any area of your body, but the most common places it can manifest are the solar plexus, heart, forehead, neck and jaw muscles, shoulders, hands, heart rate, and breathing.

Anger will manifest in one part of your body more than the others. Let your awareness go to that area where anger is strongest. Pay attention to the sensation you feel in that part of your body. Don't interfere with it; just watch it, observing its exact location, intensity, and what the sensation feels like. Is it a constricting or tightening feeling? Is it thumping or pulsing, hot or cold, tingling or numbness? Whatever the sensation or its intensity, watch it closely to see what will happen to it. This expression of anger in your body will soon change, and you need to be aware of it when it does. When it changes, you will watch to see when and how that change takes place.

In what ways can the sensation of anger in your body change? It can get stronger, or it can become softer and fade away. It can get bigger and even spread to other parts of your body. The sensation can change in any way. For instance, a constricted area might become hot, or it might relax and begin to tingle. Your attention may be drawn away from one part of your body to another. Don't resist the change. Don't resist anything. Just become aware of the sensation and intensity, and watch carefully to see how this new area will change.

If you do find yourself resisting what is happening, then observe yourself as you resist or judge. Don't try to not resist . . . only observe what is happening in your body when you do. You see? Whatever your body is experiencing, you are observing.

After your emotional body has experienced some degree of healing, your mind will again take over. It may be drawn back to the cause of the anger you are experiencing. You might find yourself judging and condemning, feeling that you are a victim, or even start feeling sorry for yourself. This is not a problem. Whenever you become aware that you are in your mind—thinking about the situation or person that caused your anger—just easily let your awareness return to your body. Start by becoming aware of your *whole body and then the particular area where your anger is manifesting most strongly, and continue to see how it will change.*

Soon your emotional body will have healed enough to free your mind from the overwhelming chaos caused by your anger. Although your anger is still quite strong, you are now able to experience it on a quieter mental level. Your mind is settling into the unfocused level where the mental tapes of the incident continue to play all by themselves. At this stage of the healing process, you're not overwhelmed by your anger. The singular anger tsunami has broken into smaller, choppier waves. These smaller anger waves come at you from all directions. You are still quite agitated and think often about the incident or person that has apparently caused your anger. You may find yourself reviewing the event over and over again, judging who is guilty and who is innocent in your mental court of law. It robs you of energy, productivity, and peace. You might finally find yourself saying, "I wish I could just shut off my mind and make it all go away!" That is coming. . . .

It is all quite automatic and out of your control. This is a perfect example of unfocused awareness. No matter how it feels, you are healing. You are less distraught than when you were pacing and panting around the room, aren't you? You are settling down. Now you are ready for the more refined phase of mental healing.

Experience #2: Healing the Mental Body

Begin by letting your mind wander for five or 10 seconds. During this time, become aware of what you are thinking. It is as if you're sitting in a movie watching your thoughts play across the screen of your mind. Watch this mental movie with easy attention, with a quiet curiosity. If you have ever seen a cat watching a bug crawling on a stone, you will know what I mean. He watches the bug's progression with complete, yet relaxed, attention. Whether or not he's going to pounce on the bug has not been decided. It is not an issue. Our cat is just observing every aspect of the bug's movement. If the bug moves to the right or to the left or stops, the cat's attention remains complete. It is as if the perception of the bug goes through the cat's eyes, right into his body without stopping in his mind.

Thoughts are like bugs. As you observe with easy attention, you are watching what they will do next. You do not have to trouble yourself with content. The content of these thoughts come out of the anger. So you're looking for what your thoughts are doing, not what they mean. At this point, trying to figure out what your thoughts mean is counterproductive. Introspection and analysis turn your awareness away from the emotion that needs healing. It's actually a form of escapism. So if you find your mind analyzing or contemplating, easily let your awareness return to the dominating emotion.

Once you satisfy the anger, the content of your thoughts will immediately become supportive and productive. For instance, there can be more of them or they may start to thin out; they can become momentarily more agitated and chaotic or quieter and softer. They can change direction, or they may even stop altogether. Your solitary assignment is to simply observe whatever it is they are doing. Nothing more.

Now it may happen that your mind will begin to boil up and overflow with anger once again. That just means that a little more spontaneous healing is ready to take place. If the anger or any other emotion becomes overpowering, then just shift your awareness to your body and begin healing your emotional body. The sensations in your body will dissipate more rapidly this time, and you will quickly return to healing the mental body by observing your thoughts.

Now if you don't take action to remove yourself from the aggravating stimuli, the cause of your anger, you will continually and often be overwhelmed by that anger. What does removing yourself entail? Well, that depends on what is either triggering your anger or lowering your overall sense of well-being. For instance, you may not be able to get away from your partner long enough to settle into the quieter levels of your mind. Or you may do things that increase your stress level and general level of fatigue such as overworking, overdrinking, eating poorly, or not getting the proper amount of sleep or exercise.

This process of observing first your body and then your mind until focused awareness allows you access to Eufeeling is foolproof, but you must align yourself with those forces and circumstances in your life that support health and harmony for optimal success. Rest, eat well, and get away long enough to allow your new Eufeeling perspective to take root and blossom.

This is important. If you can't remove yourself from the aggravating element, do the Healing the Emotional and Mental Body exercises and the QE process regardless. The results will be phenomenal, but they will manifest differently. To be sure, they will be a little longer in arriving but arrive they will, and with all the more joy and jubilation that comes from complete freedom from long-term torment. The only mistake you can make is to decide that this remarkable healing opportunity is not working and abandon it along with your relationship. You do not need faith, hope, or belief. You need only do this process one or two or three time a day with the attitude of the cat, complete and easy attention to what is unfolding before you.

Sooner or later your thoughts will become quieter. And when they do, you will notice that you feel better in some way, a sense of general well-being. You might feel lighter, freer, relief, quietness, or even peace or joy. That's right—you've just rediscovered your Eufeeling waiting for you under the tumult of tribulation that dominated your body-mind. Continue to sit easily with your eyes closed in QE Awareness for 5 or 10 minutes, and then if possible, lie down and rest for another 10 or 15 minutes.

You may need to repeat the QE healing experience several times in one session, especially if the precipitating incident was particularly distressing. In fact, you should repeat this several times daily if you're experiencing frequent or longer bouts of anger. Soon, your anger will substantially subside, and you will be free to unabashedly open to the mundane joys of life unencumbered by the draining influence of negative emotions.

One more point. When you realize that no person, object, or situation is the source of your anger, you are free of the emotional shackles that bind you to the illusion that there is an outside or even internal cause for your anger. Fear, the original destructive emotion, as with all other negative emotions, originates from the separation of awareness from Eufeeling. You have proven that to yourself several times earlier in this work. However, you can short-circuit your anger with a simple preemptive exercise: Let your awareness move to your body before your anger becomes full-blown and out of control. Anger may be felt in your body before you are even aware that you are becoming angry. The signals will be there, and you can learn to recognize them with a little practice. This has tremendous value as you can begin immediately diffusing your anger by healing your emotional body before you are powerless to perform rational thought and appreciate inner peace. So learn to recognize your subtle signs of anger when it's just beginning to bloom, and nip it in its proverbial bud.

You don't have to be completely free of anger to move on to the next phase of crafting a perfect relationship. Just make sure that you feel easy about yourself and relatively easy in the company of your partner. Now that you've repaired the cracks in your foundation, it is time to rejoin your partner and begin building your perfect relationship.

Eu-Communication

As we discussed earlier, when two people come together out of need, they both walk away unfulfilled. On the other hand, when two people communicate out of fullness, both give effortlessly of their Selves and walk away fulfilled. When you communicate while aware of Eufeeling, you are "Eu-communicating" and drawing from the same unbounded energy, harmony, and intelligence that created and is maintaining our world. You don't have the feeling that something is missing or suffer an emptiness that you try to fill with the adulation and admiration of someone. You're not swayed by how others think of you. You don't say yes when you really want to say no. In short, you are free to be your natural, spontaneous, and loving self.

It's time for you to return to your partner and have a conversation while you are aware of Eufeeling. It really is quite simple.

Experience #3: Eu-Communication

(Before you meet with your partner, you may find it valuable to sit down with your eyes closed. Become aware of Eufeeling, or even do QE Intention for a few minutes. While this will help set the tone for the meeting, it is not necessary.)

As you approach your partner, become aware of Eufeeling. Then become aware of any disturbing emotions you may be feeling. Become aware of your whole body and where those emotions may be manifesting. Just a momentary awareness in this way will help eliminate any latent anxiety you may be feeling. Now begin a conversation about a neutral topic, one that is not emotionally charged. Such topics might include the weather, a movie you just saw, or how your garden is growing.

As you speak, occasionally become aware of Eufeeling; do the same as you listen. Even find Eufeeling in the spaces between words. Become aware of Eufeeling while maintaining comfortable eye contact. That is, occasionally look into your partner's eyes while you are aware of Eufeeling, as this is exceptionally healing. Speak, listen, and maintain eye contact while being aware of Eufeeling.

Don't try to be aware of Eufeeling all the time. This will only distract you from the beauty of the moment. You only need to become aware of Eufeeling whenever you think of it. This is more like a gentle check to see if it's there. It is like a young child who occasionally looks up from his play to see where his mother is. Mother is always watching over her children. Eufeeling is always there, and, like the child returns to his play secure in the idea that Mother is watching over him, we return to our conversation in the fullness of Eufeeling.

We do not need to grow in love. We only need to become aware of the love that is already there. Each one of us was born of universal love. When we forget that, we begin picking through the pieces of our life trying to regain that wholeness. Once we are reintroduced to Eufeeling, our every thought, word, and deed reflects the wholeness that we are. The choppy seas of life still wash over our body-mind, but with our awareness anchored to Eufeeling, we can never be dashed on the rocky shores of relativity.

Helping Others

It often happens that only one person is aware of Eufeeling during a conversation. If you are experiencing Eufeeling and your partner is not, then results may be slower in manifesting but manifest they will. When two people are engaged in Eu-Communication, then what I call the N2 effect is operating. For instance, when two people are in Eu-Communication, you have two people times two people, which equals the power of four people aware of Eufeeling. We could call this number the harmony quotient. So two people in Eu-Communication have a harmony quotient of four. On the other hand, one person aware of Eufeeling speaking with another person who is not has a harmony quotient of one (1 x 1 = 1). Two people communicating without awareness of Eufeeling, or in common consciousness, have a harmony quotient of zero. Maybe I should call that a *disharmony* quotient of four . . . just kidding, but certainly interesting to ponder.

The point is that if you're the only one aware of Eufeeling, changes will most likely take place slowly. The utter joy of two people together in Eufeeling is diminished, but don't let that dampen your spirits. You are still creating a powerful healing environment, far more than if you weren't aware of Eufeeling and actually adding to the disharmony.

So what can we do to help others who are not aware of Eufeeling? Nothing. I mean that in the absolute sense. There are a number of things we can do, but there is nothing we can do for them. We can create an environment that encourages healing, but they are responsible for allowing healing to unfold.

Your orderliness will encourage them to heal, but the healing may not unfold the way you think is should. When you bring a magnet in close proximity to iron filings sprinkled on a paper, the filings go through a good deal of shifting and reshuffling before they finally array along the magnetic lines of force. Likewise, there may be a good deal of readjusting before perfect harmony finds a home in your relationship. Your best bet is to enjoy Eufeeling for yourself and let your family, friends, neighbors, and partner take care of themselves. Oddly enough, this is the fastest, simplest, and easiest approach to the perfect relationship.

What more can you do? How about doing Remote QE, Remote-Emotional QE, or, my favorite, QE Intention. Any of these procedures will quicken the pace of healing and harmony in your life, and you don't need anyone's permission to do it. Remember, that's because you're not doing anything to or for someone else. QE is always Self-exploration, Self-awareness, creating a powerful healing environment within and around you. But that is only an invitation for others to join the fun. They must make the final decision themselves, and that is much more likely when you're settled in the bliss of your own Eufeeling.

A Quick Review

Experience #1: Healing Your Emotional Body

- Sitting with eyes closed, become aware of the upsetting circumstances.

- Identify the dominant negative emotion.

- Become aware of your whole body.

- Become aware of the area of your body most affected by this emotion.

- Observe this sensation closely to see how it will change.

- Continue to observe the changes as they manifest.

- After some time observing the body, you will find yourself back in your mind.

- Return to the body until you feel that your mind has quieted sufficiently.

- You are now ready for to heal your mental body.

Experience #2: Healing Your Mental Body

- Sitting with your eyes closed, become aware of what you are thinking, as if you were watching a movie.

- Observe with an easy but clear awareness.

- Observe the number and intensity (including emotions) of your thoughts.

- Watch closely to see in what ways they change.

- Soon thoughts will become slower, quieter. This feels good.

- Become aware of that good feeling: your Eufeeling (stillness, lightness, a sense of expansion, peace, joy, bliss, and so forth).

- Watch to see how your Eufeeling will change. When it slips away, easily find it again.

- Continue lightly observing Eufeeling for five to ten minutes or as long as Eufeeling effortlessly dominates.

- Return to activity slowly, or lie down and rest.

- You are now ready for Eu-communication.

Experience #3: Eu-Communication

- Easily become aware of Eufeeling while listening and speaking to others.

- Maintain comfortable eye contact while aware of Eufeeling.

- Enjoy Eufeeling in the silence between the words.

- Eufeeling will come and go. Don't try to hold on to it; just become aware of it from time to time.

- Have no expectations. Just let your Eufeeling meander in and out of your conversation until you are finished.

PART III

QE APPLICATIONS FOR EVERYDAY LIVING

CHAPTER 28

Sleeping and Insomnia

Falling asleep is a natural, beautiful process. I say *natural* because when conditions are prime, you only have to lie down and do nothing, and sleep comes. I like activities that involve doing nothing. When mastered, sleeping makes you feel great. You have more energy, you think more clearly, and you also look better (at least some of us do).

Here's a hint for those who sleep pretty well but would like to get a little more rest out of a night's sleep. When you get into bed, just before lying down, do Quantum Entrainment for two to five minutes. It's a wonderful way to dissolve the superficial stress picked up during the day. It also allows your body to discard those tiny knots it's been tying all day and puts your mind in neutral, resetting your internal sleep meter to *aahhhh!* When you're finished, just lie down and drift into the heavenly bliss of deep sleep.

For many, however, sleeping is hard to do. I used to be one of those people, but now I sleep like a baby. (Maybe that's not the best comparison, as any bleary-eyed parent of a newborn can tell you.) There are all kinds of reasons why individuals don't sleep well, such as consuming stimulants, eating poorly, and not getting enough exercise. Jet lag, hormonal imbalance, and other medical conditions (pain or mental/emotional stress, for example) can also interrupt sleep patterns.

The list is a long one, and it doesn't seem fair that something as vital and enjoyable as a good night's sleep can be so easily disturbed. Insomnia is a symptom, and if you are sleeping poorly, make sure you find out why and fix it. If you drink too much caffeine, cut back. If you need more exercise, get off the couch and walk around the block. If you can't fix the problem or even figure out exactly what it is, then it's time for QE.

One of the most common causes of sleeplessness is emotional stress. Sometimes you will know exactly what's bothering you, and sometimes you won't have a clue. QE works beautifully in both cases. Since QE harmonizes your whole being, it is perfect at getting into those hard-to-reach corners of your mind where undiscovered stress hides. For general stress, I recommend that you do QE throughout the day. You can do it a minute at a time or for longer periods (as much as 10 to 30 minutes). My favorite time for Extended QE is first thing in the morning, as it really sets the tone for the day. And done just before bed, I believe that QE helps balance hormonal activity, including the melatonin secreted by the pineal gland, which regulates your internal night/day clock.

Getting to sleep and staying asleep can be a real problem—especially when something is bothering you. Maybe you had a fight with your boss or are struggling to pay the bills. Or perhaps your teenage daughter just got a tattoo of all the members of her favorite heavy-metal band up both arms and around the neck, culminating in the grand finale with the drummer's crossed sticks perfectly aligned in the center of her forehead. She says she'll love the band forever . . . and you wonder why sleep eludes you.

Stress can kick the mind into overdrive. Thoughts blur like the whirring blades of a fan, and you can hear yourself begging for just a few minutes of blessed mental silence. Now is the perfect time for QE, as it quiets thoughts simply by observing them. You've already experienced the no-thought state of pure awareness and how thoughts softly gather around your Eufeeling. This will work in times of stress as well, but differently.

When you're in the thick of a stressful event and do QE, you'll find the experience somewhat different from when you are more settled. It's all very relative. When your thoughts rattle like machine-gun bullets on a tin roof and you begin QE, you might find that your thoughts punch holes in your awareness. Your thoughts run away with your awareness, and QE is forgotten—sometimes for many minutes. If this happens, that's fine. Even though you don't feel as settled as at other times, a great amount of healing is still taking place. You'll see that you'll recover from the incident far more quickly than you otherwise would have. In QE, you take what you get. It will always be far better than if you hadn't done QE in the first place.

What you don't want to do is make feeling peaceful a goal. As you already know, this creates a polarity, which pulls you in two different directions. Yes, it's great to feel peaceful and free of discomfort, but working in the direction of peace is still working, and that is opposed to peace. All that is needed is simple observation. Watch and wait. When you turn off the electricity to a spinning fan, it still takes time for the blades to come to a full stop. And so it goes when you do QE in the midst of great agitation. Emotional stress is like the electricity that spins your thoughts. QE turns off the stress, but it takes time for the whirring thoughts to slow and stop. Just do your QE with no expectations, and you will really be amazed.

Of course, doing QE while you aren't agitated or under pressure is money in the bank. Then when the stress hits the fan, you will only be inches from pure awareness and the soothing influence of your Eufeeling.

Helping Others

QE can truly help others get a good night's sleep, sometimes in just a few minutes. If you share a bed with a restless sleeper, just reach over and place your hand on his or her forehead, chest, or back; and then do QE. It won't be long before the person's breathing becomes deep and regular. Even if your partner does not fall sleep right away, a deep rest will be enjoyed just from the QE. Of course, QE is made to order for helping people suffering from lack of sleep due to illnesses.

Children who have a hard time settling down to sleep or who wake with nightmares respond exceptionally well to a gentle session of QE. When you are comfortable with the QE process for yourself, you can even read the little ones a bedtime story while you do QE.

CHAPTER 29

Waking Up

For many people waking up is not so pleasant, especially if an alarm clock is involved. It is the time that waking consciousness reclaims the body and mind from the illusory world of dreams and the blissful unconsciousness of deep sleep. Waking consciousness prepares us for the onslaught of the day ahead. Too little sleep, overeating or drinking too much the night before, or distaste for the day ahead—most often experienced when we have a job we don't like—makes this first activity a negative one. This is not the way we were meant to wake up.

Waking consciousness should be embraced by the nurturing tones of peace and a quiet anticipation for the day ahead. A few minutes of Quantum Entrainment can give you the perfect start to each and every day. Here's how it is done:

As soon as you become aware that you are waking from sleep, stretch, yawn, and gently sit up in bed. Become aware of what you are thinking, and watch your thoughts as you learned to do, waiting for your Eufeeling with quiet anticipation. You will find that it has been waiting for you. Easily observe your Eufeeling for a minute or so. Now let your mind slowly go forward to the coming events of the day. As each cluster of thoughts come and go, allow your awareness to return to your Eufeeling. Do this for five minutes or so, creating a peaceful and vibrant beginning to the day.

CHAPTER 30

Brushing Your Teeth

Brushing your teeth QE style begins with a slight pause before putting toothpaste on your toothbrush. In that still moment, find your Eufeeling. If it's not there with your eyes open, close your eyes and watch your thoughts until they quiet down and Eufeeling arrives.

Now put the toothpaste on your toothbrush and become aware of your Eufeeling. Start quietly, gently brushing your teeth while aware of Eufeeling. Pay attention to how the brush feels in your hand. How do the bristles feel against your gums and between your teeth? Note where your tongue is positioned in your mouth and how the paste feels on it. What do you taste? Every time you switch your attention to another part of tooth-brushing, pause momentarily to find your Eufeeling and then continue.

After two minutes of gentle brushing, rinse your mouth and feel the swirling water playing over your tongue and teeth. Now you are ready to face the day with gentle awareness, peace in your heart, and let's not forget, pearly white teeth. Could life get any better than this?

CHAPTER 31

Eating

Most people pay little attention to the actual process of eating. We look on it as a necessary activity that is pleasant enough but often takes us away from other activities such as our work. In the U.S., we tend to eat on the run, gulping down mouthfuls of burgers and burritos, steering with our knees while careening down the highway. We focus mostly on the quantity and convenience of food rather than the quality, ambience, and process of digestion.

Nutritionists maintain that most diseases and conditions of the body are caused by, or complicated by, poor digestion. "Well," you might say, "I don't have any control over my digestion. I swallow my food, and digestion takes place automatically." On the contrary, I'm here to tell you that you *do* have a good deal of control over your digestion, and Quantum Entrainment can play a pivotal part in the process.

First of all, digestion begins in the mouth. Chewing and mixing your food with enzymes starts the digestive process. Chemical messages are sent from receptors on your tongue to your brain, telling it about the kind of food in your mouth. Your brain tells your stomach to prepare for food.

A lot goes on in the mouth, and chewing is a very important part of digestion and assimilation. If you don't break food down to almost liquid status, it may not be properly digested and cause all kinds of problems . . . from allergies to eczema, fatigue, arthritis, emotional disorders, and so on.

I have a habit of watching people eat. I know it's a bit weird, but the physician in me seems to come out in restaurants. I am forever surprised by how little chewing goes on. I'll watch diners take a full bite of a burger, cheeks bulging, chew three or four times, then raise their chin toward the ceiling and swallow. You can actually see the congealed mush of wilted lettuce, pickles, white bread, and meat chunks work its way down the gullet like the vanquished prey of a boa constrictor. My, what we do when we choose not to chew!

So how can QE help with eating and digestion? QE creates balance. A proper-functioning digestive system, like every system of the body, must be in balance to operate free of malady. Doing QE for 30 seconds before you eat will set the tone for your meal. It will slow you down so that your digestive system can prepare for the food to come. It will encourage you to chew longer and more slowly. But if you don't seem to be able to remember to take 30 seconds before a meal to do QE, then just do it as you're preparing to eat. Become aware of your Eufeeling, and then allow your mind to think about the meal to come. If you like, you can do QE Intention that the food will nourish and support your body-mind in every way needed.

If you have a digestion-related condition, you can do QE at any time. For instance, if you've finished your meal and your gall bladder has left you bilious and nauseous, reach for a handy-dandy bottle of QE. You'll be amazed. Symptoms like nausea, burning, and gas can be quelled in minutes . . . maybe even in seconds! I had a client whose stomach blew up like a balloon every time he ate. It was accompanied with pain and gas, and the symptoms kept him from enjoying a dinner out on the town. The first time we did QE, it took several minutes for its effects to be noticed. But slowly at first, and then more rapidly, I could actually see his distended stomach melt like butter on a warm skillet. As his belly got smaller and smaller, his smile got bigger and bigger. Mine, too: no more gas.

My client learned QE, and now he does it for himself. His condition is improving remarkably and so is his state of mind. Today he goes out to eat whenever he wants, enjoying both food and friendship.

QE affords not only a deep, healing rest for your body, but it also exerts a harmonizing influence over your emotions. Emotions such as anxiety and anger have a negative impact on your digestive system, but QE balances them. A quiet mind is paramount for both effective digestion and assimilation.

Just because we eat something does not mean that the nutrition contained within that food will be assimilated into our cells. Eating while in a hurry or emotionally agitated has a devastating effect on whether or not nutrition reaches our cells. Consuming a meal under stress can cause ulceration of the stomach lining, constipation or diarrhea, gall-bladder and pancreas problems, torsion of the bowels, inflammation of the pockets and folds of the intestines (diverticulitis), and so much more.

Although it's often overlooked, the process of eating is vital to overall health and productivity. We usually think of nutrition as something that is good for the body and mind, yet even our social interactions are profoundly affected by what and how we eat and the way in which it is digested and assimilated. I strongly suggest that we do QE before, during, or after a meal—or all three. What have we got to lose but a little dyspepsia?

Try this exercise out at the table. You will be amazed by the effect it has on every aspect of eating, including your sense of wholeness and well-being.

Eu-Eating

Eating while aware of Eufeeling soothes the tummy and the soul and allows for greater enjoyment of an activity we routinely take for granted. Here's how to do Quantum Entrainment while you eat:

Before taking a bite, begin by doing QE for 30 seconds. Let the aroma of Eufeeling waft up into your awareness. Now begin eating. Watch attentively as you use your fork or spoon to bring a morsel of food to your mouth. Feel the texture of the food as it lies on your tongue. Set the spoon or fork down, and briefly find your Eufeeling again. This should only take a second, as the Eufeeling will be quietly waiting for you. Start to chew and pay attention to the flavor and aroma of your food. Identify the different smells and tastes (salty, sour, bitter, sweet, astringent, pungent), and see if you can tell when each arrives. Chew until your food is almost liquefied and then swallow. Find your Eufeeling, and then note the taste that is left on your tongue.

You may not wish to do this for your entire meal, but doing it for even a single bite will greatly enhance your health and dining pleasure. A good rule of thumb is to do

QE eating completely for at least three morsels per meal. Of course engaging in Eu-eating for the whole meal would be absolutely divine.

Helping Others

First of all, dining with peaceful partners will go a long way toward helping everyone relax while they're eating. If the person you're eating with is shoveling down food as if he were in a contest at the county fair, and if he isn't open to doing QE himself, then your QE will help him slow down. Even though QE isn't an energy technique, it creates wells of positive, soothing energy around anyone who does it. This soothing energy will work its way across the table to the offending diner. During the course of the meal, he will quiet down and act more appropriately. If you find that his obnoxious behavior isn't responding fast enough, then just get up, walk around the table, place your hand on his forehead, and do QE. This is guaranteed to get him to stop eating, if only momentarily, and he'll most likely get the point.

By the way, the more aware you are of pure awareness, the more peace you generate. But don't be fooled by thinking that peace is a barometer for awareness— it isn't. The Bhagavad Gita, which offers answers to virtually all the general problems facing humankind, warns that you can never tell how evolved someone is by observation of outward appearances or how you feel in the person's presence. However, insufferable behavior at the dinner table is a pretty good indication of a lack of awareness.

Of course, you can also help others by doing QE to improve eating habits and alleviate symptoms. Remember that you don't need to get permission to do QE for anyone at any time. This is simply because you aren't doing any-thing. You are only becoming aware of awareness and then watching to see what happens. Your intention won't work if it is, in any way, harmful to someone else or the environ-ment. You are free to QE your little heart out on anything you like. In fact, I encourage it.

CHAPTER 32

Hunger and Overeating

For most industrialized countries, hunger and starvation is extremely rare. But it will not take much in the way of climatic changes, war, pestilence, or famine; and even the most affluent nations will find its citizens without enough food to sustain their needs. The QE process can be an exceptionally positive influence on hunger and even starvation.

Individually, if you are hungry, you can do QE, and the pangs of hunger will be reduced or eliminated in a very short time. It also quickly relieves the emotional attachment to food, and for this reason is even helpful for those people who eat too much.

Obviously, QE Awareness does not take the place of food, but it does greatly slow down the metabolism so we burn fewer calories and need less food to survive. An additional benefit to doing QE while hungry or starving is its effectiveness at fulfilling our desires on the material plane. QE Awareness has a very powerful harmonizing influence on the environment. It brings to us opportunities and material possessions, including food, in a way that is beyond the linear thinking produced by our minds. When we do QE Awareness, all the creative forces of the universe rally around our needs and desires.

QE for hunger should be done in short sessions of three to five minutes. Sitting quietly is best, but this can be done under almost any circumstances, including while working, during a conversation, driving, exercising, and so on.

QE for starvation should be done continually to conserve energy and other vital resources of your body. Sitting up is the best position, but QE will also be effective while lying down if you are too weak.

CHAPTER 33

Midday Rejuvenation

Throughout the day, we take a respite from the rigors of our work with coffee and lunch breaks and occasional banter with our co-workers around the watercooler. While these breaks give our minds and bodies respite from the constant pressure of our jobs, they are relatively useless for the deeper rejuvenation that has proven so deeply valuable for those people who do QE in the workplace. Doing Quantum Entrainment sometime during your busy day will reap great benefits for you (and even your employer), such as clearer and more creative thinking, increased stamina, less absenteeism, and a friendlier, more supportive attitude toward co-workers. There are two ways to do this, with eyes opened and with eyes closed.

The QE midday rejuvenation is best done with eyes closed in a secluded spot, like a private office or in your car during your lunch break. Once you find a quiet place, simply close your eyes and watch your thoughts until your

Eufeeling greets you. Then continue to do QE with your eyes closed for ten minutes. That's it!

If you can't find a place to close your eyes, then sit quietly with your eyes open and look at any object. Then do QE and enjoy your Eufeeling. Find another object to look at and return to your Eufeeling. Do this for ten minutes or so accompanied by your Eufeeling as your eyes move around the room.

Of course, the QE midday rejuvenation works just as well on your day off. Try it. You will be amazed.

CHAPTER 34

Computer QE

It's easy to get sucked into that time sponge we call the computer. Many people spend hours staring at their monitor, which leads to eyestrain, stiff joints and muscles, and foggy thinking. QE is perfect for computer work.

Here's what you should do: Sit comfortably erect with shoulders and arms relaxed. Frequently pause and find your Eufeeling. Then continue what you're doing in this way: imagine the words and pictures as coming out of the monitor and into your eyes and mind.

Normally, we do the opposite. We feel that we're leaning toward and looking into the screen. This gives us a feeling that we are working, moving out of ourselves and into the computer. When we do QE and allow the words and images to come to us, there is a shift in perception that feels like we're not working, as if the work were coming to us. The result is a more relaxed, clearer thinking computer operator. That's you.

Don't forget to take a break every 20 minutes or so, and do QE for a few minutes with your eyes closed.

CHAPTER 35

Falling Asleep

Now that the day is ending, you have one more chance to enliven your awareness and treat yourself to the nurturing influence of your Eufeeling. By doing this simple exercise, you will relieve the stresses built up during the day and prepare yourself for a good night's sleep.

Just before you are ready to go to sleep, sit up in your bed and watch your thoughts easily and with attention. Your Eufeeling will soon arrive, ready to tuck you in. Settled in the gentle awareness of Eufeeling, let your mind lazily review the day's events. Watch your earlier experiences play across the screen of your mind like a movie; and when there is a break in your thoughts, become aware of your Eufeeling again—thoughts and Eufeeling, Eufeeling and thoughts, flowing across your mind like clouds on a sunny day.

Do this exercise for five to ten minutes, and then slip down under the covers and fall into a deep and restful sleep . . . good night.

CHAPTER 36

Talking

Most people talk in order to convey some information, but the deeper value in talking is communicating who we are underneath the words. Below everything—our thoughts and emotions, our likes and dislikes, our hopes and fears—is our basic nature.

You already know who you are. Your true essence is Eufeeling. Traditional communication is superficial and does not include awareness of Eufeeling. Talking to another while aware of Eufeeling enlivens deeper meaning and love, making communication with someone else full and fulfilling. Here's how to deepen your communication with others.

When you greet people and prepare to speak with them, become aware of your Eufeeling just as you start. If you pay attention during the conversation, you will recognize your mind making notes about the other individuals or even judging what they say or who they are. This is a perfect time to become aware of your Eufeeling. Do so at every opportunity while you converse. If it doesn't make those you are talking with uneasy, maintain a comfortable eye contact while being aware of your Eufeeling. In this way, you will feel more relaxed and giving, and those around you will feel a sense of ease and trust. In most cases, everyone will walk away feeling more fulfilled.

CHAPTER 37

Walking

Walking is so automatic, we rarely pay much attention while we're doing it. QE brings grace and flow to the stately art of walking. Here's how it's done.

First place your weight evenly on both feet, shoulders squared with a relaxed upright posture. Take a nice deep breath in, and as you exhale, allow your mind to gently find your Eufeeling. If you need to, close your eyes and attentively watch your thoughts until your Eufeeling appears. Now you are ready for QE walking.

Before you actually take a step forward, imagine that you are the unmoving center of the universe. Instead of you walking through your world, see the world coming to you. Even when you actually start walking, imagine that the plants and people and buildings are coming to you. In your mind, they are in motion and you are stationary. Objects come into view, then slowly slip past your field of vision while your legs appear to effortlessly rise and fall in place. One more thing: when objects come into sight, imagine them as coming from nothing, as not existing until you see them. As they pass out of sight behind you, see them dissolving into nothing. And when you pay close attention to that nothing, you will discover your Eufeeling smiling back at you.

You can do QE walking anytime: in your house or office, through the country or the winding streets of the city. Soon you will find that walking has become an effortless, flowing joy full of fun and enlivening awareness.

CHAPTER 38

Space-Walking

Walking is excellent for rejuvenating the body. Our beating hearts and circulating blood infuse our tissues with energy-giving oxygen and remove the toxins that cause physical and mental discord. What most people don't realize is that walking can be an excellent exercise for our other heart—the one we often refer to as the *soul* or *spirit*. I call this *space-walking,* and the benefits go far beyond a traditional stroll in the park. Let me explain. . . .

To the casual passerby, space-walking looks the same as plain old everyday one-foot-in-front-of-the-other walking. But inside the space-walker, the symphony of the spheres sings in perfect harmony with the sparrow's song, the wind through the grass, the beating of every heart of every created being. Sound impossible? Not at all. Space-walking is not only possible, but it is also easy once you know how to do it.

As we navigate through our daily routine, our senses remain engaged by things, and our minds are consumed by thoughts. For instance, when we enter a room, we note the objects that occupy it. We see the coffee cup on the table next to the couch on which Aunt Tillie is blissfully stretched out, enjoying her afternoon nap. But there is something in the room of great value, and it rarely gets noticed: *space.* That's right—simple, all-enveloping space.

When we pay attention to space instead of the objects that define it, something very magical begins to take place: Our minds slow down, and our bodies relax. Then we begin to see the world in a most beautiful and wondrous way. Our lives are forever and incredibly enriched simply by acknowledging space. Here's why:

Both saints and scientists tell us that all things come from nothing.

When we become aware of nothing, we travel back to our birthplace as it were. Coming home nurtures both body and soul. It feels good and—as we'll see in a moment—is so good for us.

Space is *not* nothing. It is simply the emptiness between two objects. Space can contain air, radio waves, odors, dust mites, water vapor, and so on. But to the mind, space represents nothing, so we can use space as our gateway to bliss and harmony. Let's lace up our walking shoes and learn how to space-walk.

Start out with a gentle walk in pleasant surroundings. As you do so, begin to notice not birds or cars or plants, but rather, the space between those things. Find the space between the trees, between the branches, and then locate the space between the leaves. Don't look at the clouds; look into the vastness between the clouds. Anywhere you see two things, note the space between them.

You can use sound to find space as well. Listen to the even fall of your feet on the ground, and then find the silence—the space—between your footfalls. Listen to the distant whine of a siren. Listen intently until the siren finally fades into silent space. Space is everywhere. You only need to become aware of it to begin space-walking.

Are you getting the idea? Good. Now you're ready for the final step. This is the most important part of space-walking. Once you find space, don't look at it as if it were just another object to be identified. Your mind will become quickly bored if all you do is identify it. The mind likes stunning vistas and juicy problems to sink its mental teeth into, and space is neither of these.

Here's the trick—the magic of finding your soul and filling your heart: Once you find space, peer intently into it as if it was a thick fog, and you're waiting to see what will come out of it. Look into the depth and breadth of every space, and pay close attention to not only what you see, but also to what you feel. That's right. Find your Eufeeling in the space between two objects. It will melt your heart.

Observing space is easier to begin with, but as your mind becomes more infused with pure awareness, it will feel equally at home with space or substance.

Start space-walking slowly and become more active as you learn how to hold the silence within the space. Many people will actually do QE before space-walking. This has the advantage of reminding the mind of the space between thoughts. It's a short step from there to see and feel the space between things.

See how many activities you can introduce space-walking into. Consider space-working or space-cooking or even space-brushing your teeth. Have fun with it, and do it often. In time, it will become effortless. Then you will be the one who's holding back tears of joy.

Helping Others Learn to Space-Walk

You can teach others how to space-walk by going with them and describing what you are doing. Make sure they are quiet to begin with, and keep idle chatter to a minimum. You may even start with a QE session at home before you venture out. If you really want to have fun, take a group space-walking. Pure awareness is more easily realized in a group. Eliminating idle chatter in a group is almost impossible, so plan some silent time followed by short discussion periods. Groups of three to eight are good. If you have more participants, break into two groups.

This exercise is especially valuable for children. If you take out a group of youngsters, encourage them to talk about their experiences as they occur rather than waiting for a formal discussion period. Children naturally take to the spaces and may even teach you a thing or two about the joys of space-walking.

CHAPTER 39

Listening to Silence

Hearing is the only sense that is working all the time in every direction. For this reason some say that it is the most important sense. It keeps us in touch with our environment 24/7. If a child's cry or suspicious noise is heard, it can even wake us from a deep sleep. Sound has two parts: the vibration that triggers hearing and silence. Our minds focus almost exclusively on the sound and miss the beauty and benefit of silence. Listening to silence will fill your life with stability and stamina, and an easy peace that will be there even in the midst of a cacophony of sound. Make the following simple experiences a part of your daily routine, and you will find your life deeply enriched.

When you hear any long-lasting sound like a bell toll, train whistle, or a siren, listen until the very point it drops below your hearing threshold. As soon as the sound disappears, there will be silence. Then listen attentively to only that silence, and you will find a good feeling—your Eufeeling—waiting for you.

When listening to music, easily become aware of the silence between the notes. Go from silence to silence, letting the notes fade into the background. Soon you will appreciate a deeper fullness of the music while peace and harmony sing in your heart.

While walking, become aware of the sound of your feet as they hit the ground. Then become very acutely aware of the silence between your steps. As you listen closely to that silence, become aware of how it makes you feel. Presto chango, Eufeeling!

CHAPTER 40

Smelling Your Eufeeling

Our sense of smell has been much underrated. It does in fact have a very powerful influence over mood and motivation. The right smell can clear our mind, lighten our spirit, and make us feel almost giddy. The sense of smell is also intoxicating in another way: it is a direct path to Eufeeling.

Find an aroma or fragrance that you enjoy, such as coffee, chocolate, or a flower. Inhale slowly and deeply through your nose, and note the texture and flavor of the smell. After you inhale, hold your breath for a brief moment until the smell diminishes then dissipates. As soon as it disappears, it will be replaced with "no smell," a gap between smells. Easily become aware of this gap, and pay attention to how you feel. Of course you will find your Eufeeling waiting for you there.

Now gently exhale while continuing to be aware of your Eufeeling. Get in the habit of doing this with any smell you encounter throughout the day. It even works to diminish the negative impact of obnoxious odors. QE smelling is a delightful and effective way to inner peace and outer awareness. So tune up your nose, and get sniffing.

CHAPTER 41

Mood Monitoring

Intermittently monitoring your emotional status throughout the day will create a more fluid, relaxed, and peaceful you. QE mood monitoring is a powerful tool to eliminate unproductive emotions, replacing them with naturally supportive and creative ones. In the beginning you will have to remind yourself, via a timer or sticky notes, to check in and see what emotions you are experiencing. After you've done this exercise for a while, it will become natural. Here's how to do QE mood monitoring:

During any normal activity, become aware of how you are feeling. You may be bored, irritated, frustrated, anxious, content, happy, or excited. The idea is to simply identify what you are feeling, and then watch that feeling to see what happens. Remarkably all feelings have Eufeeling at their root. So when you quietly observe any feeling, you will soon arrive at your Eufeeling.

If you're experiencing a very strong emotion, then you will be overtaken by it. You only need to wait until it quiets down a bit and then innocently watch it until it finally dissolves into that quiet, always-positive Eufeeling. If you are negative, don't try to change what you are feeling. Let your Eufeeling do that for you. You just need to watch the negative feeling without trying to do anything, and miraculously your Eufeeling will shine through and lighten your day.

CHAPTER 42

How to Be Creative

Does anybody have any idea where ideas come from? How about a hint? Ideas are thoughts, right? And thoughts come from . . . pure awareness. Thus, ideas come from pure awareness. Ideas are a form of creativity, and so they must necessarily come from the source of all creation. It stands to reason that if you want to become more creative, then it would be good to get close to pure awareness.

Let's have a short review of some of the principles we discussed previously. Less action (rest) is the springboard for more action. We see this principle being played out all around us, but we usually just focus on the action part. For instance, we sleep and then perform an activity. Our hearts beat after the rest phase, our eyes blink and open, and there is a pause between every in and out breath. The Earth rests in winter, and I wonder if the expanding universe will some day reverse itself and contract back into complete and utter awareness.

Another principle of rest and activity is apparent: the deeper the rest, the more dynamic the activity. The most obvious example is sleep. When sleep is shallow and restless, we don't perform our best the following day. We can also interpret this principle in terms of direction by saying that when we want to exert an influence in one direction, we must start by going in the opposite direction. We normally don't look at life in this way, but simple inspection will show it to be apparent.

If, for instance, you want to get up from the chair you're sitting in, what is the first action you perform? You push down with your hands and feet in order to stand up, right? If you want to build a skyscraper, then you start by digging a hole. If you want to drive a nail, you start by drawing the hammer in the opposite direction. If you want to shoot an arrow toward a target, you must first pull it in the opposite direction.

If you want to build a bigger skyscraper, drive a nail deeper, or shoot an arrow farther, then you must dig a deeper hole, raise the hammer higher, and draw the arrow farther back. You can imagine what would happen to a 20-story building if the foundation were only ten feet deep.

Pure awareness is the deepest rest you can get. Awareness of pure awareness will afford the most dynamic activity. Pure awareness is also found in the opposite direction of any activity. Remember that pure awareness in nonactivity, so it's always less than any activity you perform. The deepest rest and the most dynamic activity come from being aware of pure awareness.

All of this is pretty obvious and intuitive, but we seem to completely miss this principle when it comes to creativity. Our minds most usually chug along in a very active manner. We fire off one thought after another, day after day, year after year, until the body-mind finally dissolves back into the ocean of awareness from which it was born. All during our lives, we pay little attention and less homage to pure awareness and its role in creativity, and yet there is no creation or creativity without it.

We become more creative in the same way we shoot an arrow. When we shoot an arrow, we draw it back, back, back until it is fully drawn and at rest. At this point the arrow is nonmoving but full of potential. Now, what does the archer have to do to get the arrow to the target? All he has to do is aim and relax. Once the arrow is fully drawn, at rest, and properly aimed, all the forces of physics rally to support its unerring flight to the heart of the target.

Creative ideas issue forth from the consciousness of a mind fully drawn and at rest in pure awareness. The consciousness of a chaotic mind is slightly drawn, and resultant thought and activity is weak. We don't have to look too far to see how common our senseless, irrational, hurtful deeds have become. Acting from a chaotic mind is like pulling an arrow back only a few centimeters and letting it go. The arrow falls pathetically at the feet of the ineffective archer.

All this talk about ideas and weak thought and going in the opposite direction to find fulfillment is all well and good, but does it have any practical value? Yes! We can become more creative, or actually allow creativity to flow through us more effortlessly, when we are aware of pure awareness. Thankfully, we already know how to do that. A little tweaking won't hurt, however. Let's take a closer look at how to inspire more creativity in our lives.

How to Plant the Seed of Creativity

This is a pretty short procedure, so don't blink . . . but you can sit comfortably with your eyes closed. Review all the pertinent points involved in the situation before you do Quantum Entrainment. For instance, if you have writer's block, can't find the right color for your canvas, or are lacking the musical notes for your stalled opus, let your mind run over what you are interpreting as failure. See clearly where you are stuck and then let it go.

Now sit down and do QE. Watch your thoughts as they refine and finally disappear to be replaced with your Eufeeling. Continue to observe your Eufeeling and it will become fuller. Now, while you are completely wrapped in your Eufeeling, have a thought of what you want to create. Just produce one single, simple intention, image, or idea; and then step back to watch what happens. For instance, "Opus complete" or "Canvas full of color." Once is enough! Don't muddy the clear waters of pure awareness. A single, subtle intention while fully aware of the Self is absolutely all that is needed. Then watch and wait.

One of two things will happen: either the solution will present itself immediately and you're done, or nothing will appear to happen. If you don't receive an answer right away, stay in that fullness a little longer if you like. Contrary to those who believe that creativity is born of suffering, creativity blossoms in the fullness of the Self. If you decide you must cut off one of your ears, at least do QE on the way to the emergency room.

Since creativity flows from your Self, take time to get to know your Self. Increasing creativity is far more effective when Extended QE is performed. Five, ten, or even twenty minutes will help. With extended times, there is no need to repeat your intention, but you may find your mind lazily examining the problem from different directions. Don't initiate this examination. Let it take its own course. Remember not to interfere; just watch. The solution may present itself slowly, but almost always, it's revealed in a flash of insight and almost never how or when you expect.

If creativity doesn't arrive immediately, then the seed-thought you dropped into the sea of pure awareness while floating on your Eufeeling is still germinating. It is organizing, rallying all the forces of creation around your concerns. The answer is coming; you just need to wait and watch, whiling away the time with your Eufeeling. If it doesn't arrive in this session, take a break and do another session later.

This is a foolproof method of revving up the creative juices, but in the beginning it may take time, mainly because your mind keeps trying to make something happen. I can guarantee your answer will come, but never as expected, so lighten up and hang out. If your answer did come as you expected, then you wouldn't be creating anything, would you? So once you drop your question into the fertile soil of awareness, don't bother with it again. Continually checking your intention is like digging up a seed every day to see if it's germinating. It will never grow if you continually disturb it. Just sit back and enjoy the delight of a day on the ocean of bliss.

When will creativity come? Sometimes it will arrive bundled in the light of recognition right away, and sometimes later that day or the next. When you get good at not looking for an answer, it will come almost immediately.

When to Plant the Seed of Creativity

The active mind is planting seeds all day long. We call them desires. If we listen to our mental chatter long enough, we will find it full of judgment and desire. On the superficial and weaker level of the conscious mind, many thoughts are directed at what we want and how to get it. That is because at that level we are isolated from awareness of pure awareness and look outward for fulfillment in things, people, events, and ideas. No matter how strong the desire at this level, the action will be weak and fulfillment of the desire is not realized. Or it is realized only after a great deal of work and willpower.

The mind settled in pure awareness has few desires other than those that are beneficial for all. The word *desire* is really too strong. These impulses are more like preferences. Rather than feeling, *I'd really love to have that red sports car,* the settled mind would think, *Nice,* and be able to enjoy it for what it is, without a need to own it. This approach saves on car payments, gas, and insurance. So right away, many of the strong desires that your active mind has are satisfied simply by slipping below the waves of chaotic mental activity and dwelling in the depths of pure awareness.

If you enjoy artistic activities such as painting, music, writing, and dance, you're already familiar with being in the "zone." With QE, you can overcome those frustrating times when your art suffers from diminished creative flow. In writing, this is called writer's block. I've never had it. I sometimes get tangled up with how to say something or just don't feel like writing, but when I sit down, I can write. Why? I let the content flow from pure awareness through my Eufeeling, and then "me" just records what is there. If you're in a creative slump, do QE daily and often; and then become more active than usual. Walk or go dancing, and then sit silently and do QE. You'll be quite surprised by the way in which your creative juices will begin flowing. You may need to carry around paper towels to soak up the excess juice.

If you're working on a math or engineering problem, the mechanics of creativity are the same. Become familiar with the particulars of the problem and then leave them for the quiet orderliness of Eufeeling. The annals of science and technology are fraught with examples of discoveries by individuals who found solutions to their problems while daydreaming or when just falling asleep. For example, it was Friedrich August Kekulé, the discoverer of the benzene ring, who for months had been trying to figure out its molecular structure. He finally gave in and sat exhausted in his chair before the living-room fireplace. His mind now free from imposed effort, he watched as the flames lazily curled and licked at the crackling logs. Then, in that silent state, the answer came to him. He watched as a flame curled around itself like a snake swallowing its tail. *Aha!* thought Kekulé. *Benzene is a ring.* And so it was.

It was in his quiet mind, settled in orderly stillness, that the answer took form and wriggled its way up into Kekulé's disinterested consciousness. He was fortunate to have been sitting in front of that fire under those circumstances. You are far more fortunate. You have QE. You can visit pure awareness and wallow in the fullness of Eufeeling while the forces of life hasten to do your bidding.

So remember, when you come up against a stubborn problem of any kind, review the problem, then do QE. When you're aware of your Eufeeling, easily intend that the solution be forthcoming and then wait disinterested in that fullness for the answer to appear.

Helping Others Overcome Creative Blocks

And if others are having a creative crisis, you can offer to help. Just have them think about what they want to accomplish, and then you do QE. The best scenario may be an Extended-Remote QE session, but that is completely dependent on personal circumstances. Remote or other-wise, Extended QE will probably be the fastest road back to free-flowing creativity. You will notice your own creativity opening up as well.

CHAPTER 43

Problems with People

No two people are the same. No two people see the world through the same eyes. Even identical twins perceive the world from different vantage points, have a different intellectual and emotional capacity, have different physical abilities and health challenges, and have different hopes and dreams for their future. It is the differences that define us one from the other. It is that which is the same within us all that will bring us together. Eufeeling, at its most subtle manifestation, is the same for us all. Awareness of Eufeeling encourages unity between people, families, and countries.

When you see people as a source of disharmony, know this: the disharmony comes from within you, not from the actions of others. What they are doing may be wrong, but your negative reaction does nothing to help the situation. As they say, "Two wrongs don't make a right." QE has the perfect solution for negative thoughts toward others, and here is what you can do:

Become easily aware of the other person's offending activity. Do this for 5 to 10 seconds. Now become aware of your reaction to this behavior. Do this for 10 to 15 seconds. Finally, become aware of your Eufeeling, and enjoy this awareness for one to two minutes. Settled in your Eufeeling, let your mind drift back to the vision of the offending activity and then how you have reacted to it in the past. Aware of Eufeeling, allow your thoughts to alternate between the activity and your reaction. If you find yourself judging or creating additional disharmonious thoughts, this is just a different reaction to the behavior. Continue to watch whatever rises in your mind with simple innocence while settled in awareness of Eufeeling. Do this for two to three minutes.

When can you use QE to quell disharmony between people? Anytime at all: with people causing trouble during public transportation, disagreeing with a boss or co-worker, disciplining children, handling noisy neighbors, and here is an emotional biggie . . . giving guidance for elected officials, to name a few.

When unaware of Eufeeling, we focus on the differences between us and others. This is a divisive perception that is healed through awareness of Eufeeling. We don't use Eufeeling as a tool to fight against negativity; we don't use it for anything. Simple awareness of Eufeeling without a thought of what must be done will bind the wounds of our fragmented society.

CHAPTER 44

Improving Athletic Performance

I very much admire what athletes can do with their bodies. I've played sports all my life and love the feeling I get when I'm challenging my body to perform. I love working on a skill in practice only to witness as it is spontaneously and flawlessly expressed during competition. The athlete also has to maintain a highly tuned psychological game. I know the hardship it places on the psyche when a magnificent athletic body is injured—in fact, most athletic slumps are more mental than physical. Quantum Entrainment successfully addresses both mental/emotional and physical problems. And of course, QE is invaluable for the completely healthy athlete as well.

Putting Your Self in the Driver's Seat

What does it mean to improve athletic performance? It means to enhance coordination between body and mind.

But what does coordination between mind and body mean? And why do we need a body in the first place? Silly questions? Let's take a look.

Most of us live in a world that isn't too physically challenging. We don't have to climb hills, trap game, and throw spears in order to survive. We learn most of our survival motor skills when we are young, then coast the rest of the way. But athletes have chosen to up the ante by pushing their bodies, honing them into finely tuned precision instruments.

Athletic performance starts in the mind, the container for all thoughts. We look outward into the world through our senses. Sensory impressions come into our minds and are processed; and then, if we decide to execute some necessary action, our bodies respond to fulfill that action. Of course, this is a gross oversimplification, but it will do for our purposes here.

The mind is like the driver, and the body is like the car. Your body is the vehicle for your consciousness. It drives it around so that your consciousness can experience through the senses and increase your relative knowledge of the world you inhabit. When consciousness is ego driven, you're motivated by fear and can't really enjoy the ride. It's like driving in traffic when you think that every car is trying to hit you. When your Self is in the driver's seat, however, your body and mind are relaxed and easily reactive. So it is also with athletics. An athlete settled in the Self is also relaxed, and spontaneously responds physically. You will hear a Self-centered athlete say about his or her performance: "I was in the zone. My body performed flawlessly, and I was perfectly calm."

When athletes are Self-aware, they are fluid and free flowing. They are less likely to injure themselves. They often feel as if their bodies are on automatic pilot. Playing Self-aware is an effortless delight and one of the greatest joys of life.

Many athletes turn professional for the wrong reasons. They see a chance to do what they love and get paid for it. But if they fail to cultivate Self-awareness outside the playing field, they will inevitably focus on fame or fortune, and the joy of performing is soon lost. They burn brightly and then burn out. The softness of Self is traded for the hellish hard life of sharp edges and straight angles. In this aspect, QE offers balance, harmonizing the personal and professional life while protecting the joy that playing brings to an athlete's heart.

The following is a story of one such athlete. Julian has maintained his exuberance for life and his excitement for his sport in the very competitive and stressful arena of professional tennis. Julian is from Germany and plays in a 35-and-over league. But that was all threatened when he sustained a knee injury while playing fatigued under trying circumstances. Here is Julian's story in his own words:

> I am a professional tennis player in the over-35 league. At the end of the year, I felt burned out and very tired. It was then that I hurt my knee playing tennis. I tore a ligament and couldn't touch the ground with that leg. I treated it with ice and anti-inflammatory drugs. After a week of treatment, however, the knee was no better, and my doctor wanted to do an MRI on it. That week, I met Dr. Kinslow. He

did a QE treatment on my knee for about five minutes, and immediately, I felt a little better. When I asked for more sessions, he told me that I would be able to do it myself. After reading a copy of his book <u>The Secret of Instant Healing,</u> I started doing QE on my knee.

After only a couple of days working on my knee, I experienced my Eufeeling. Every time I did QE, my knee felt better. I knew my knee was healing itself. I practiced QE daily, and after 40 days, I was completely free of pain. Now I'm playing in tournaments—and winning—and I have no problems with my knee at all.

But there is a bigger benefit from working on my knee. Ever since I learned how to use QE, every part of my life has gotten better. I find immediate peace whenever I need it. Since I'm a professional athlete, I rely heavily on an inner calm and peace in order to bring out the best in me. Since using QE, I'm able to feel that flow nearly on a daily basis. But this summer, I started having a fluid and flowing experience like never before. While competing in tournaments, I had incredible peace and strength that let me reach new heights in my playing . . . and brought me tremendous inner joy.

Julian not only overcame the physical damage to his knee with QE, but he also realized that the joy he felt while performing when he was Self-aware could be realized off the tennis court. As he continued to be Self-aware, he found that QE improved his competitive edge astonishingly. In 2007 and 2008, Julian became the European champion, and in 2008 he defeated the best player in the world in his age group.

Julian is living the vision I have for all athletes: Self-healing within *and* outside of their athletic endeavors. But the vision goes beyond this. Whether we are athletes, computer wizards, CEOs, or store clerks, integrating QE into our lives must necessarily raise us above the struggling human condition and free us to naturally be who we are and do what we love.

CHAPTER 45

Physical Stress and QE

In times of natural disasters, you may be called to perform unusual feats of strength and stamina. Helping to remove the rubble of a collapsed building or walking a long distance with little food or water will place great demands on your body. The QE process creates a very deep level of rest in a very short time. Rest, as you know, is the universal healer. The deeper the rest, the deeper the healing. QE provides the body with a deeper rest even than sleep. (While QE provides the body with a deeper rest than sleep, it is not a substitute for sleep.)

The remarkable thing about the QE process is that you don't have to stop your activity in order to receive healing rest. QE can be done during activity, helping to heal the body as soon as stress and injury occur. Then when you finally do get a chance to rest, do QE for an even deeper healing experience. The value of QE for athletic injuries is unquestionable. QE is fast, effective, and noninvasive. It does not hurt to apply and cannot create any further insult to the injured tissue. It's perfect!

Increasing Energy and Endurance

When a burst of energy is needed, whether lifting a boulder or a barbell, begin the physical feat and then become aware of which muscles are contracting. As you continue to strain against the load, become aware of Eufeeling. You may notice that you are aware of Eufeeling and your contracting muscles at the same time. This creates a unique condition, something like a relaxed contraction where your muscles feel relaxed even while they maintain a heightened contraction. You will also notice at this time an inner peacefulness as if your body continues to work hard while your mind is watching comfortably from the couch.

When a longer-lasting energy is needed, like a distance run or a sustained march, do QE as often as you think about it. Be not only aware of Eufeeling within the mind but also find it in your body and the things and spaces around you. QE will greatly reduce the tedium and trauma of sustained activity.

CHAPTER 46

Acute Injuries

Let me start out by reminding you that QE should never be substituted for proper medical care by a licensed health-care professional. However, QE should always be used to support and accelerate traditional emergency procedures.

While Quantum Entrainment is not itself a healing technique, it has proven to have a remarkable influence on the rapid healing of acute pain and injury. We have seen it work wonders for sprains, strains, ruptured spinal discs, headaches and dizziness, and shock from trauma, as well as the emotional confusion, depression and despondency caused by personal loss. No matter what the trauma or condition, QE should be applied quickly and continually, along with the proper treatment, until the injured is out of danger. Then continue QE until the injury has healed.

QE will work equally well whether or not you can touch the injured person. If you are providing the treatment during an emergency situation, then you can do QE intermittently as you get the chance. You do not have to direct healing energy or have an intention about how healing should take place. The QE process takes care of all of that for you, automatically and without effort. All you need to do is the QE process and become aware of Eufeeling.

Healing and harmony begin immediately without any further effort on your part. Your main challenge will be to not try to force healing to take place. Increased activity and the anxiety that accompanies emergency situations may find you trying to force QE as if it were an energy technique. This won't work! If you find yourself trying to hold on to Eufeeling or trying to make healing happen, don't try to stop it. Just observe that you are trying, and the thoughts of effort will soon fade away. There you will find your Eufeeling.

CHAPTER 47

Traveling with QE

Some people find traveling fun, while others find it inconvenient or even terrifying. Let's look at this more closely to see how Quantum Entrainment can help make travel more exciting, fulfilling, and effortless. While I will first focus on traveling by airplane, any of the QE tips for air travel can be applied to travel by car, boat, train, foot, donkey, and ostrich . . . to name a few. If you enjoy air travel—or at least tolerate it because it gets you where you want to go quickly (most of the time)—then here are a few QE tips to make the event easier and more fun.

If you're traveling across time zones, you are vulnerable to the phenomenon known as jet lag—a disruption of your circadian rhythms, which are regulated by a tiny area of your brain in the hypothalamus called the "suprachiasmatic nucleus." Now you can take this information and stuff it in your ear for all the good it will do you, but I thought I'd show off my ability to Google "circadian rhythms."

I do know this: when I travel by air—especially across time zones—I QE most of the time. Typically, I won't read, engage fellow passengers in conversation, or look out the window until I've had my fill of QE. I just love the quiet and peace and full feeling I get, but the real bonus is when I reach my destination more refreshed and—after a stretch and a yawn—am ready to take on the world. When you travel beyond your home your body is under more stress to adapt to the increased and unfamiliar sensory and abhorrent energies affecting it. If you are walking, your body has time to adapt to the new environment. Traveling by car puts more demand on your body-mind to adapt to the quickly fluctuating sensory input. Traveling by air has a much greater destabilizing effect as you pass through these energetic areas of influence. They tug and pull so quickly that your body-mind is continually kept off balance. Flying across time zones adds the additional stress of perverting your circadian clock.

Thus, doing QE while you fly—and, to a lesser extent, while you drive—will keep you in relative harmony with the imposed stressors as they impact your body-mind. Being aware of pure awareness creates a kind of superconducting, frictionless flow that allows stress to pass around and through you without interfering with the normal functioning of your nervous system, cell metabolism, or thought processes. Traveling still takes effort and energy, but at least you are keeping the harmful influences to a bare minimum. If flying causes you anxiety, then QE is made for you. Have a good long Emotional QE session before you leave for the airport, while waiting to board, and all the while you are on the plane. Remember, do not turn away from your fear, but look at it easily while you are aware of pure awareness. Peace or stillness or some other manifestation of your Eufeeling will grow in your awareness, and anxiety and fear will fall away.

If you become airsick, then QE will help there, too. You may initially find that the nausea will get stronger for few minutes. Stay with it, as healing is taking place, and soon you will be able to control the nausea with awareness alone.

When traveling by car, QE can be a great comfort. I rarely drive with the radio on. I love the silence and find pure awareness a friendly and supportive passenger. And not once has it told me that I'm driving too fast or that I just missed a prime parking spot like a wife I know. (Not you, honey. I was thinking of another wife who does that.) Get used to driving aware. Once you break the "gotta have sound" habit and turn off the radio, you'll love the fullness of silence that surrounds you.

Speaking of parking spaces, try QE when looking for one or when you're stuck in traffic. Just have the easy intention for a clear space or for the traffic to yield to your intention, and then forget about it from there. More often than not, you'll be surprised by how well your Eufeeling works things out for you.

Helping Others

When you know QE, helping others travel makes it easier for them and more fun for you. Of course, you'll have to be on the lookout for excuses to don your cape and tights and appear as QE Man (or QE Woman) to save the day. The most common problems noted in an airport, for instance, are travel fatigue; irritability; and the "I'm late, I'm late, for a very important date" syndrome. You can help your fellow travelers with Remote QE. And you can do the same for your family and friends via light touch or remotely if you like. Are the kids getting a little restless? QE is the answer!

Have to go the restroom but can't get out of your seat? QE! Hungry, bored, or sick? QE, QE, QE! Just think QE first, and then everything else. QE always helps, never hurts, and feels so good.

CHAPTER 48

Overcoming Fears

Do you have a fear of flying, crossing bridges, or even leaving the house (agoraphobia)? Before you have to leave the house, cross the bridge, or fly, sit down, close your eyes, and do QE for 10 to 15 minutes. During that time allow your mind to imagine the upcoming activity. Just let you mind look ahead for a few seconds, and then return to your Eufeeling. Do this for a few seconds every minute or so throughout the QE session. When you are engaged in the actual moment, pause every now and again and become aware of Eufeeling. If you are traveling, frequent short sessions are better than longer ones, but both will work. If your phobia is very strong, then do a few practice runs before the real deal. One important point: Don't keep checking to see if your fear is diminishing. Instead, enjoy Eufeeling and accept whatever comes to pass.

At a Quantum Entrainment workshop in Germany, I met a woman who had flown in from her home in Asia to attend the workshop. Now this by itself is not unusual; our workshops enjoy a stimulating assortment of people from around the world, but she had a different story to share.

This woman told me that she suffered from severe ago-raphobia. She could not leave her apartment. If she even approached the front door, the opening to the outside world, she would become immobilized by fear. She would shake violently, become deeply nauseous, and have an immediate bout of diarrhea.

At one point, she read my book *The Secret of Quantum Living* and learned how to do Quantum Entrainment for herself. As she practiced QE, she noticed that she could get closer to her front door without experiencing those debilitating symptoms. Soon she could open the door; and one fine day after many years of confinement, she stepped across the threshold into the outside world. She continued her QE practice, moving farther and farther from her home and staying away for longer periods of time. When she heard that QE workshops were being offered in Europe, she bought a ticket for Hamburg . . . and you know the rest of the story.

There is no disharmony that can ultimately overshadow awareness of your Eufeeling. The harmony of Eufeeling is all pervading. Given time, patience, and practice, you can sur-mount even the most intimidating and frightening obsta-cles, one QE session at a time.

CHAPTER 49

Driving

Most of us drive without being aware of what we are doing. Isn't that true? Our minds are usually elsewhere while we perform the mechanical process of driving our car. While the radio plays in the background, our minds wander aimlessly from one topic to another. When we arrive at our destination, we were barely aware of driving and most of the time can't even remember what we were thinking about, or traffic was an ordeal that left us frustrated and angry. There is, however, another way to drive that offers a much more fulfilling experience. Doing QE while on the road not only increases our awareness of what we are doing, but also adds greater pleasure to the joy of driving.

Next time you get into the car, turn off the radio and listen to the stillness. Find your Eufeeling in that stillness. As you begin driving, observe the road and other cars as if moving through the stillness of your Eufeeling. While watching the road, become aware of your hands on the steering wheel. Feel the muscles contract and relax as you turn the wheel. Find your Eufeeling. Don't focus on your destination. Leave early enough and drive in the slow lane, enjoying the journey and your Eufeeling. You will be amazed that you will arrive at almost the same time as if you drove quickly, cutting in and out of traffic. QE driving will get you there refreshed and at peace.

Driving in Heavy Traffic

Travel always requires extra effort and at times can be downright traumatic. Here are a couple of ideas on how to apply QE in heavy traffic. . . .

When you find yourself becoming agitated or anxious, become aware of Eufeeling. You may immediately lose awareness of it, but that will soon pass. When it does, you can return to your Eufeeling again. Don't try to keep your Eufeeling, just easily wait for it to return. Continue to do so, and you will find that the harshness of heavy traffic will soon soften.

Slow-moving traffic, detours, and other delays can present significant challenges. When you find that time is moving but you are not, QE can help. Find your Eufeeling and have a quick thought, something like, *arrive on time* or *clear and easy travel.* Now just sit back and enjoy the ride. Don't look for any changes, as this may have the opposite effect. Just let the forces that be do the driving.

Looking for a parking space? Likewise, have a fleeting thought for a space, listen closely, and then release it. That is the secret to success: Have the thought, and then sit back and enjoy. Can't just let go? Then do QE for emotional disharmony.

CHAPTER 50

Teaching Our Children QE

The mind of a child naturally and easily moves toward awareness of his or her Eufeeling. This becomes less evident as children grow up, however, because of the influence of their control-oriented parents, teachers, and even their peers. As kids get older, they forsake the complete helplessness and freedom of infancy for the ability to manage and organize the things and people in their environment. They must learn to live within imposed boundaries. This growth is necessary and good, as everyone must learn to be self-sufficient in order to become Self-sufficient. It's necessary to give in to the pressures of adulthood—that isn't the problem. The problem is that once we've learned how to control our lives, we must go on to reclaim the lost joys of childhood—the natural awareness of our Eufeeling.

A child left on his own will perish. He must learn to survive. Once those skills have been mastered, that child becomes an adult. To complete the cycle of life, that adult must then revisit the magical realm of childhood and become reacquainted with his Self. There, the two halves become whole: the inner child has grown up and the adult becomes more childlike. The sum total is freedom expressed within boundaries, which is the best of both worlds. In essence, we can have our cake and eat it, too.

As adults, we still aren't finished growing. What we call adulthood is more like an extended adolescence. It is the adults of this world who have, well meaning or not, led us to this precipice on which we find ourselves viewing the insidious crumbling of cultures, the falling away of our very humanness. We are capable of unbounded love and infinite intelligence, yet they are rarely expressed. Out of ignorance or sloth, most adults do not return to embrace the purity of their childhood.

This is the second most-grievous crime an adult can commit. The first is to keep our children in ignorance of their Self. All the ills of humankind—and I mean *all* our ills—would vanish in a generation if our children could only learn to become free adults fully aware of their inner essence, seated in the nurturing arms of Eufeeling.

I am offering you that choice. Teach your children—teach every child you know—the simple rules of Self-awareness. Continually remind them of the basic joys surrounding them, the timeless radiance of their Eufeeling. Give them a chance to become free now, and the choice of maintaining that freedom into adulthood. Let them learn that the Self is the permanence permeating all change. Give them the greatest gift they could ever receive, and then stand back and watch as peace quietly descends on Earth.

Kid's QE

The ages at which children can learn QE will vary, depending on the child. At what age you begin to lead your children inward will depend on their temperament, talents, life experience, and emotional maturity. You can start preparing your little ones as soon as they can identify their own feelings. If your child is very young, you may need to help him or her learn to differentiate between positive and negative feelings before introducing "Kid's QE." This is especially valuable for the male child whose culture may encourage him to repress his emotions in preparation for manhood. Once children know which emotions they are feeling, they're ready to learn Kid's QE.

Just as you learned to follow your thoughts inward to the silent level of your mind, so will you guide your children step-by-step to consciously appreciate their own expression of the quiet joy of their Eufeeling, their inner essence. The overall idea is to get your kids to turn their attention inward for short periods of time. It's good to nurture their awareness when they are playing or performing routine activities so that they can readily identify what they are feeling at any given time. Depending on your child, this takes time, and it shouldn't be rushed. Just the process of becoming aware of his or her body or thoughts and emotions is very settling and will quickly lead to Eufeeling.

Do an activity that elicits a positive reaction in your child—happiness, excitement, laughter, and so forth. This could be a favorite quiet activity such as reading a story; playing with toys; becoming aware of his or his body and how it works; or just soft, interactive conversation. Reading aloud *Martina and the Ogre*, a vividly illustrated children's book offers a wide range of interpersonal interactions and emotions that are excellent avenues to your child's inner world. (The DVD and CD are available in English through the QE website at **www.KinslowSystem.com,** or you can find the story without illustrations in the chapter called "Children" in my book *The Secret of Quantum Living*.)

It's best to begin with something that your child is already familiar with on a sensory level and move inward from there. For instance, let's say that you're sitting on the floor with your son, and you have him hold out his hand and look at it. Then you lightly brush your fingers across his little hand and ask him how it feels. He might say, "Ticklely!" and giggle. Then ask him how it makes him feel on the inside. He might reply, "Happy," and smile broadly. You've gently taken his awareness from out to in. Now he is ready to become aware of deeper, more silent reaches of his mind and the complete stillness of Eufeeling.

Calming emotions like happiness and love are a good place to start. Once your little one is feeling a positive emotion, ask him to describe it. Then ask him to be very quiet and look at or feel the emotion to see what happens. This is a subtle and important part of the Kid's QE process. The child needs to watch the feeling to see what it will do next. You can tell him that he is a cat and the emotion is a mouse, and say: "Watch very closely to see what the mouse will do next." Just as with your learning experience, it is your quiet attention that discovers Eufeeling. Your child will soon learn to become still in body and mind.

Do this for up to ten seconds, as a child's mind will want to wander to other things. Then after some brief conversation, bring his awareness back to his good feeling. Point out that when he closely watches his feeling, he begins to feel quieter or more still or happier inside. His awareness is refining, moving from an emotion to the deeper, more stable stillness and peace of Eufeeling.

Then point out to your child, "When you quietly watch your good feeling, do you see how it makes you feel quiet and happy inside?"

Ask him to watch his happiness or stillness or peace or whatever Eufeeling he is having, and then describe what happens. He may describe what he is thinking or sensing, or tell you a story. Let your child talk for a while, and then have him pause. Ask him if his good feeling is still there. He will likely say yes!

Ask him to again watch his good feeling, and point out how it makes him feel happy inside. Tell him that this is his *Happy Place*. It is his special, secret place. He can go there anytime he likes. He can visit his Happy Place when he is tired or angry or afraid. It will always be waiting for him like a good friend.

At first, just do short learning sessions together—a few minutes at most. Very soon, you will only have to remind your child to "go to your Happy Place," and he will easily become aware of his Eufeeling. Eventually, your child will come to realize that his Happy Place is always there, whenever he wants it. He'll carry this joy into adulthood and, as a loving adult, share that love with the rest of our Eufeeling-starved world.

I recommend that you sit with your children for one or two minutes several times a day while they quietly go to their Happy Place. If they start talking, let them finish and then remind them to silently return to their Happy Place to see what is happening: to watch carefully and observe any changes. Very soon they will go to their Happy Place on their own or simply when reminded. It's best if they do not close their eyes. This will help them recognize their

Eufeeling even while they are playing and interacting with others.

As they grow, they can do Kid's QE for longer periods, but generally, shorter, more frequent sessions are most beneficial. Later, when they are 10 or 11 years old, as their bodies and minds mature, they can close their eyes and explore the deeper reaches of their silent minds. It will be the perfect meditation, and they won't have to learn a thing. They can do their Kid's QE with eyes closed once or twice a day. A good rule of thumb is for them to do the eyes-closed Kid's QE for as many minutes as they are old. For instance, a 12-year-old would do Kid's QE with eyes closed for 12 minutes, one or two times a day. They can go to their Happy Place as often, and as long, as they wish with their eyes open.

Introducing your children to their Happy Place is the single-most important tool you can give them. You will find the radiance of their inner light shining on their faces and the awe of the mysteries of life reflecting in their eyes. They will carry that joy into adulthood, inspiring other adults to find *their* Happy Place.

This will be the blossoming of the most precious seed, which you lovingly planted in your child's heart so many years ago.

CHAPTER 51

Helping Children Manage Stress

The fragile emotions, frail bodies, and delicate nervous systems of children are quickly compromised by stressful conditions. They are completely dependent on their parents and other adults to protect and nurture them. QE allows a parent to do both.

- Regular and deep sleep is vital for an emotionally and physically sound child. Two minutes of QE at bedtime erases the concerns of the day and makes for a deep and nourishing sleep. If your child has bad dreams or is afraid of monsters under the bed, QE will quell his fears and show him that his Happy Place is stronger than any monster.

- A physically exhausted child responds immediately to the soothing presence of QE awareness.

- Children struggle to find their center and are easily upset if their routine is broken and things don't go as they expect. QE quickly balances their emotions, showing your children that outer stability comes from their Happy Place within them.

- Teach your child to find his Happy Place and do QE for himself. Make sure the next generation has the best start in a world of immense challenges.

CHAPTER 52

Loving Our Pets

Our pets are adopted members of our family. To varying degrees, they depend on us for the creature comforts like food and shelter. But a pet is more than a possession. They thrive on our attention and loving care. They are remarkably sensitive, by human standards, and drink in our kindness like pure sunshine. Eufeeling, the result of deep peace generated by QE, is the purest sunshine you can offer your pet.

Humans and animals are capable of forming deeply fulfilling relationships, often stronger than relationships among humans. It is almost as if we and our animal friends were made for each other. In fact, I believe this to be true, as animals reflect back to us purity and innocence. They are like spiritual tuning forks that help us vibrate in a higher, more loving realm—in return, we enliven a deeper sense of self-awareness in them.

Quantum Entrainment for animals is done in the same way as for humans. Around the world, every pet, from horses to horned toads, has found relief for everything from tumors to arthritis, to behavioral disorders, and ingrown toenails. Whether done remotely or by human touch, your pet will benefit deeply from your QE sessions. And don't do them just for symptomatic relief. You can engage in a quick, five-second QE session whenever you touch your pet or look into its eyes; and save the longer two-to-five minute sessions for times of bonding. Do Quantum Entrainment before walks or training and during feeding. Look at Eufeeling as a common ground between the species, a place where you and your beloved companion can meet in total innocence, joy, and love.

CHAPTER 53

Dealing with Bad Weather

When it comes to the weather, we are quick to point out, "Everybody talks about it, but nobody does anything about it." This is a reflection of the impotency we feel when it comes to controlling the weather. Control it? We are hard-pressed to even predict climate beyond a day or two. Indigenous peoples often endeavor to control the weather through prayers, chants, and ceremonies with limited results. Industrialized man doesn't even try. He considers himself fortunate if he remembers to take along his umbrella.

While we have had many reports from ecstatic QEers who have apparently stopped the rain and wind, raised or lowered the temperature, and quieted turbulent seas to their own amusement, I know of no one who does it consistently. It would make an interesting field for research, and although the potential to control the weather with QE is there, I think we will focus our efforts on what we can immediately control: our reaction inclement weather.

When you are exposed to a harsh climate, your body will work hard to maintain homeostasis. If you are hot, cold, or dehydrated, it will go to great lengths to keep you within normal physiological parameters that will allow you to go on living. When you do QE, you do not have to understand what the body is doing. You introduce harmony and healing from the finest functioning level of your mind outward into your body. Your lungs will remove toxins and oxygenate your blood, and your heart will pump that blood with perfect precision, nurturing all your bodily systems. In other words, doing QE gives your body its best chance to adapt to severe climatic changes.

But that's not all! QE will dampen the negative effects that bad weather imposes on your mind. For instance, it is one of the best treatments for the depression-like symptoms of seasonal affective disorder (SAD) caused by insufficient sunlight.

CHAPTER 54

Clean Water and Healthy Plants

It has long been known that our thoughts and emotions have a marked effect on our environment. Quantum physics tells us that our environment is a reflection of our thoughts and emotions. There is well-established research to show that both positive and negative thoughts intimately affect the growth of plants and even the molecular structure of water. That makes our thoughts very important indeed. No matter where in the world we go, we will find that most people are entangled in the unending web of common consciousness—that is, unfocused, weak, and scattered thinking. The opposite of common consciousness is QE Awareness, which contacts a thought at its conception deep within the mind, not on the superficial surface. Thoughts that grow from QE Awareness are strong, vibrant, and harmonizing.

It is the disharmonious thinking of common consciousness that is responsible for the pollution of our waters and the poisoning of our plants. It takes only a little QE

Awareness to neutralize the damage that has been done. Here is how to do QE for clean water and productive plants:

> *If convenient, touch the plant or hold the water in your hands. If that is not possible, then look at or imagine the forest or body of water in your mind. For instance, you may live in Europe, but you can imagine the widespread burning of the rain forest in Brazil. Touch the plant or water with your hand or hold the image in your mind, and become aware of everything that you can perceive. Do this for about 30 seconds. Now aware of your Eufeeling, create a QE Intention. While aware of Eufeeling, allow your awareness to easily move back to your perception of the water or plant. Do this for three to five minutes or as long as you like.*

If you have ways of testing the reaction of the plant or water after your QE session, you might find it interesting to do pre- and posttests. If not, you can rely on your senses, taste, smell, and sight to give you feedback. Sometimes the changes are dramatic and recognizable in a short period of time. I have a papaya tree that was in shock a week after transplanting. Its leaves were drooping and falling to the ground. I gently touched the tree and did QE for about two minutes, and 20 minutes later the leaves had deepened in color and were reaching proudly toward the sun. You may also notice the taste of water improving.

The potential for purification is profound, but be smart. (Do not ingest toxic plants or water even after doing QE unless you absolutely know them to be safe.) Doing QE to cleanse our environment has immediate purifying effects both on the environment and on the minds that caused the problem to begin with.

CHAPTER 55

Insects and Other Pests

Civilized humans have effectively isolated themselves from nature. In doing so we have lost a good deal of our natural immunity to insects and other pests.

Whether you find yourself living on the street or just out for a weekend camping trip, QE can help overcome the annoyance and even danger of everything from insect bites to snakebites. (You can also refer to the section on acute pain in Chapter 46.)

> When bitten by an insect like a mosquito or a wasp, do QE immediately. Initially the itch or pain may get temporarily more intense. This is an indication that healing is taking place. Shortly thereafter, the pain or itching will subside as your body begins to function more efficiently and the toxins are neutralized. If you are allergic to bee or wasp venom, make sure you do QE immediately and continually while being treated for the bite. The decreased blood gases,

increased cardiac output, and capillary dilation along with decreased fear and anxiety all help your body neutralize the venom and deal with the symptoms of anaphylactic shock. The same QE procedure should be followed with snakebites or any other animal bites.

The QE process can even be used to keep pests away from you and your house. If you have ants or termites or other invaders, do QE once or twice daily with a quiet thought that the invaders will leave. If you find yourself the main course of a mosquito smorgasbord, then do QE with the idea that they will no longer bite. Many people have been successful at removing pests from their homes and assaulting their bodies. I am what my friends call a mosquito magnet. They will take me on camping trips, not because they think I have a sparkling personality, but because all the bugs are busy biting me, leaving my *friends* bug-free to enjoy the great outdoors. As for me, QE has helped only marginally to keep the little varmints away, but it has been a great comfort neutralizing the discomfort of mosquito and other insect bites.

CHAPTER 56

Instant Peace— Watching the Watcher

Everyday living can be hectic and unsettling. Anything can happen at anytime, disrupting your life and creating a sense of unease and disharmony. No matter what happens, you will need a way to quickly become aware of Eufeeling even under the most catastrophic circumstances. Here is a profoundly effective three-step process that will do just that:

While performing any activity, become aware that you are doing so. Watch the activity as it unfolds before you. Then become aware that you are watching yourself watch the activity. This is the "watcher of the watcher," an expanded awareness that is watching you while you are watching what you're doing. Now become aware of what you feel when you are watching the watcher: stillness, peace, awe, joy, bliss. This is your Eufeeling waiting for you to discover it in the expanded awareness of watching the watcher.

It is a common spiritual teaching to watch the watcher, but you can deepen this experience extraordinarily by becoming aware of Eufeeling. Your mind will quickly become bored with just awareness of this indistinct watcher. When you become aware of your Eufeeling in the watcher of the watcher, it lightens the soul and enlightens of the mind. It is the final and necessary step that opens your awareness to the joy of being fully human.

CHAPTER 57

Group/World Peace

It is a mistake to think that we must have hundreds of thousands of single-minded people actively protesting and practicing world peace for world peace to become a reality. In fact, the opposite is true. Certainly we can see that we are no closer to world peace despite the concerted efforts of millions of good-intentioned people over the last 100 years. World peace will never be realized by outward actions alone. It first needs the support of inner peace, and that's where QE comes in.

Because of a natural phenomenon that has been referred to as the N^2 effect, it takes only the square root of 1 percent of a population, be it photons or human beings, to create a spontaneous shift from chaos to coherency. This observable fact was dramatically demonstrated by the Transcendental Meditation group in the 1970s. They reduced the crime rate by an average of 24 percent in 22 major cities in the United States simply by having a sufficient number of meditators daily experiencing deep inner peace in that city. We don't have to understand the science to get world peace. It is much simpler than that.

We need little more than 8,000 people practicing Quantum Entrainment at any single time to overcome the chaos of this world and supplant it with a less destructive, more productive one. What might you expect from this more coherent planet of peace? A QE world encourages harmonious individual expression within the group. In other words, the individual's needs, desires, and hopes will support and be supported by the needs, desires, and hopes of the group: the family unit, cities, states, and countries. What can you do to tip the scale toward world peace? I'm glad you asked. . . .

- Every hour on the hour do QE. It doesn't matter if you do it for a second or a minute; at the top of every waking hour, let your mind easily entertain the peace of Eufeeling. You will be doing it with thousands of other QEers around the world, and in a few days you will be amazed by the changes in your own life.

- Become a member of the QE Forum. There you will find others of like mind where you can share ideas and QE healing sessions and join a QE world-peace group. You will find the QE forum at: **www.KinslowSystem.com.**

- Practice QE for yourself and others as often as you like. The most potent power for world peace is your own peace. Your individual harmony will be added to the thousands of others around the world, and with no more effort than that, world peace will dawn.

How to Host a Group/World Peace QE Session

There are many ways to do a Group/World Peace QE session. You can let your imagination be your guide and have great fun doing it. I will give you a basic outline for a World Peace QE session.

Begin by asking everyone to sit in a circle facing each other. The initiator is also the timer. Moving clockwise, each person will speak out a deep personal desire in a word or phrase. For instance, if one member wanted healing for a serious disease so that she could live free of pain and worry, she may say simply, "Health and happiness." Once everyone has a desire word or phrase in mind, you are ready to start.

- Sit in a circle facing each other.

- The initiator asks the person on his left to state a word or phrase that represents their personal desire. Everyone in the group looks at that person.

- When the desire is spoken, everyone closes their eyes and does QE for the predetermined time. Two minutes is good, but some smaller groups may do QE for five to ten minutes while larger groups may do QE for one minute.

- When the time is up, the initiator/timer says, "Next."

- Everyone opens their eyes (they must open their eyes) and looks clockwise at the next person in the group. When all eyes are open, the next person offers their desire word or phrase and then the cycle repeats itself until the initiator—the last in the group to take a turn—has given his desire.

- When the time is up for the initiator's desire, he says, "Next." Then he presents the group's desire, *world peace,* and the members do QE for the last time.

CHAPTER 58

Hosting a QE Practice Group

Quantum Entrainment is always more fun and much more powerful when shared with others. Remember the N^2 effect? Your results will multiply with the number of people you share QE with. Not only that, but QE Practice Groups also tend to foster more meaningful friendships among group members. This bonding comes from sharing on the deepest level of human interaction—the level where all differences dissolve: the level of Eufeeling.

This is your guidebook to living fully on both sides of your life: the inner and the outer. Following the suggestions and performing the techniques within these pages will ensure that you live your life to its fullest, from a depth yet unplumbed. I have introduced you to sweeping concepts and powerful practices in a gentle, clear, and practical way. You have learned how to clear your mind of thought in seconds; and do the QE Triangulation Technique, providing rapid and deep healing in minutes. You also know how to find Eufeeling, your inner essence and the hub around which all creation revolves. You learned how to do Quantum Entrainment at a distance and can use it toward physical and emotional discord, finances, relationships, athletics, travel, food, chronic illness, and creativity.

You now have the skills to positively affect every area of modern-day living. You learned to find the absolute stillness of Pure Eufeeling and there softly create a QE Intention for outer prosperity while at the same time unfolding your inner essence deep and true. You even learned how to teach children to find their "Happy Place," ensuring peace and harmony throughout their lives, into the next generation and beyond.

This book is a practical guide to happiness, fulfillment, and prosperity. It is a tool kit filled with tools that build bridges to your dreams. But there is more, for there is yet something missing that will greatly speed your success—something that will multiply your practice exponentially while adding joy and fun and camaraderie. What is that missing ingredient? Simply this: the Quantum Entrainment Practice Group, sharing QE with a group of likeminded people, either in person or remotely. The QE Practice Group is the fastest, most enjoyable means to realize the world you would create. Joining or even hosting a group is an exciting and inspiring event open to anyone. Following, I will explain more about what this is exactly and how you can benefit from it.

What Is the QE Practice Group?

The QE Practice Group is a gathering of people who meet to practice the various techniques and applications of Quantum Entrainment. They are lively, vivacious, and fun.

It is healing and harmony amplified and reflected back to you through the presence of those of like minds and hearts. It is a chance to discuss with others what you learned and in turn share with and in their experiences. In short, the QE Practice Group is a rocket ride to becoming fully human.

How Big Is a QE Practice Group?

Two or more people constitute a QE Practice Group. Obviously, the more people in the group, the greater its influence on all the members. The N^2 effect is very much in evidence with just two people doing the group outline. Imagine what benefits you will enjoy when you join a group of hundreds.

Can the QE Practice Group Be Done Remotely?

Yes! Remote QE Practice Groups are very popular and practical. It is always good to physically join other QEers when possible. There is nothing like sharing QE in person, but Remote QE Practice Groups are just as effective and for many, the only practical way to meet with others. My suggestion is to be a member of both and quadruple your fulfillment. Why limit yourself?

Who Can Attend a QE Practice Group?

To join a QE Practice Group, you must first know how to do Quantum Entrainment. There is absolutely no teaching taking place in any QE Practice Groups. The practice group is designed around engaging in Quantum Entrainment and its applications. Therefore, you must at least have learned and practiced on your own the QE Triangulation Technique and Refined QE. If you want to learn QE in a group, you must attend a QE workshop, but remember that you don't have to learn in a group.

You can learn QE by reading about the techniques in this book or one of my other books on Quantum Entrainment, including *The Secret of Instant Healing, The Secret of Quantum Living,* and *The Secret of Everyday Bliss* Or if you like to learn by listening, there are several CDs and DVDs on The Kinslow System website (**www.KinslowSystem. com**) that are excellent for this purpose. (You will find a complete list of QE books, CDs, DVDs, and other products listed at the end of this book.) So you see, I have made it extremely easy for you to learn QE for yourself. Just make sure you learn and practice the QE Triangulation Technique and Refined QE before you attend your group.

When you arrive for your first group session, it will be necessary to show up a few minutes early. Before the group begins, you will be asked to perform the basic QE Triangulation Technique on another member to demonstrate your grasp of triangulation. If you do not know the technique, you will be asked to wait to join the group until you have had a chance to learn it. So by all means learn and practice this simple system before you arrive.

As a QE Practice Group member, it is wise for you to continue reading and practicing QE between group sessions. I also encourage you to practice and enjoy the benefits of the QE 90-Day Program (more information is in the next chapter). You will find it unlike any regimen you may have done before, such as dieting, exercising, or practicing a musical instrument. This program is only successful when you don't try. It must be easy and enjoyable, or it won't work.

How Long Do the QE Practice Group Sessions Last?

Typically group sessions last from one and a half to two hours. However, shorter versions are quite common and may last as little as ten minutes. Group QE sessions longer than two hours are not recommended unless there are extenuating circumstances. There are many factors that determine group meeting time, such as the number of people, location, time of day, and so on. Ninety minutes to two hours seems to be the optimal time for QE group sessions.

Who Can Host a QE Practice Group?

Anyone who has learned the QE Triangulation and Refined QE techniques and has practiced them with someone else (in person) can host a QE Practice Group. It is of the utmost importance to understand that the person hosting the QE Practice Group is *not* a teacher but only *organizing* the group. He or she is not an authority, as there is no authority in the group setting. All members are on equal footing no matter how many books they have read or how much experience they have had doing Quantum Entrainment. It is recommended that hosting be rotated among the group members. Rotating hosts keeps the focus on the group and not the host. Remember, there are no authorities in a QE Practice Group. When I attend a QE Practice Group session, I do so as a participant; and that is because there are *no* teachers and *no* teaching taking place in QE group sessions. This is why it is called a "practice" session.

I probably should point out at this time that Quantum Entrainment is an internationally registered trademark and refers to only the Quantum Entrainment technique of which I am the only teacher. I share this with you not to toot my own horn but to alert you to those who may have decided that they can teach QE to you or others. They cannot. While QE is easy to learn, it is deceptively difficult to teach. Invariably, when an imposter tries to teach QE, they ultimately succeed in passing along with their teaching minor and often not-so-minor impurities that result in diminished lasting effects, and they can even create harm on the physical or psychological level. As my teacher used to say, "Safety first." Why take a chance with an imposter when you have easy and safe access to the real thing?

It is my dream to make QE available to anyone in this world who would like to learn it. I have made Quantum Entrainment liberally available at nominal fees through workshops, books, CDs, DVDs, and webinars. Think of it. You can learn directly from me, the discoverer and developer of QE, a technique that can eliminate pain and emotional discord in minutes and then usher in the joy of living fully aware, significantly improving the scope and quality of your life for less than $15. I will train teachers when the time is right, but until then, it is extremely easy for anyone who wants to learn QE to do so either from me personally or through my products. So QE Practice Groups only *practice*—believe me, that is where the power is.

Sometimes there can be a difference of interpretation of material among members during the group session. There is no need to be concerned. No matter what it is, don't waste time debating or trying to find an answer. This is not necessary during the meeting. Let the discrepancy stand until the next session. Between meetings you can find the answer in several ways:

- Read directly from one of my books or listen to my answer from a CD or DVD. I suggest you find two or three references to help make the point clearer.

- Go to the Frequently Asked Questions on the QE website, or view my Q&A videos on YouTube.

- Join one of our social-networking sights like Facebook or Twitter.

- Inquire about taking a Quantum Entrainment workshop online.

- Address your question to **Info@ KinslowSystem.com**. Because we answer each question personally, it may take some time before you receive an answer from us about your group session. Consider finding your answer using this option only if you have not had success with the choices above.

What Material Is Covered During a QE Practice Group Session?

During a QE Practice Group session, only QE material is practiced and discussed. There are hundreds of excellent philosophies, systems, and techniques available today; and they all have their benefits to be sure. The QE Practice Group is interested in only one system: Quantum

Entrainment. The single focus of the group is to practice QE. We savor our time during the group experience, and therefore, we *never* discuss or practice other systems.

When this rule is broken, members of QE Practice Groups become confused and frustrated. The group quickly becomes diluted and breaks down, losing the chance to enjoy and integrate the benefits of Quantum Entrainment in their personal lives. It is suggested that if some individuals wish to compare and contrast QE to other systems, those individuals do so at another venue and time outside the sanction of the group. During the session keep on topic and adhere to the following outline provided, and you will avoid the confusion and occasional harm that can result. I cannot stress this enough.

How Is a QE Practice Group Organized?

Below is the outline for a QE Practice Group session. Honor the times suggested, and you will derive the greatest value from you group session.

1. **Start with a five-minute Self or Remote QE session.**

2. **Practice section (30 minutes).**

- Read a specific technique or experience exercise from a QE book, or listen to it on a QE CD or DVD.

- Follow the directions exactly.

- Practice the process. (Do not introduce more than one technique and one experience exercise per group session.)

- Discuss experiences, results, and testimonials. (Do not socialize at this time.)

3. **Philosophy section (five to ten minutes).**
Listen quietly to an interesting excerpt from a book, CD, or DVD. Note the "listen quietly" part, as that is paramount. Don't entertain discussion during the philosophy segment. One person reads or you listen to a CD or DVD. At this point all members listen quietly until the passage is finished. Then without discussion, move on to the next session. I know this is not traditional and may seem unusual, but doing it in this way will have a very concentrated impact. Learning this way has two very significant benefits:

- Because of the previous activities, the listener is already in QE Awareness. That means the knowledge is understood and assimilated best in that comfortable silence. It is as if the knowledge is a seed that is planted in the bed of silence. In this way, that seed of knowledge becomes most fertile. It will gently and quickly bear fruit in the weeks and months ahead.

- It eliminates confusion, which can come from discussion with others who may have misunderstood the material. Without an authority there to point out the subtleties of the teaching, much confusion leading to frustration and disillusionment may ensue.

4. Group/World Peace Session (5-20 minutes).

(You will find the outline for the Group/ World Peace session in Chapter 57 of this book.)

5. Socializing.

This is a time for all to come together and enjoy each other's company. It is a time to share QE experiences, talk about family or work or just the weather. Discussion of QE philosophy and technique is okay but only if it comes up naturally in conversation. Discussion of other systems is still discouraged. This is meant to be an easy time of giving and receiving the joys of QE Awareness. Time spent socializing at the end of the QE Practice Group session is not considered part of the group time. It is a special time to share the joys of being fully human with each other.

Altering the QE Group Session

If there is a time restraint, you can abbreviate the QE Practice Group session to meet your needs. If you only have a few minutes, then just do the Group/World Peace session. If you have a half hour, then start with a few minutes of Self or Remote QE and then practice one of the QE techniques or experience exercises. You can adjust your group activities to meet your schedule, but never change the rules that guide your group, and you will always enjoy an enriching and inspiring session.

Keep in Touch

Let me know what you are doing. We love to hear about you and your QE Practice Group. We can support you and may have suggestions to help get the most from your QE group experience. Address all e-mail to: **Info@ KinslowSystem.com**.

CHAPTER 59

The QE 90-Day Program

Becoming fully human is effortless once you reach momentum—when you become aware of your Eufeeling automatically when needed. For instance, when you are first introduced to Eufeeling, even though it has been with you your whole life, it takes a little conscious direction on your part to become aware of it. This will not always be the case. In fact, in a very short time you will be aware of Eufeeling whenever you think of it. It is like putting on a coat on a chilly day. When you first put the coat on, you can feel its weight and warmth. After some time you forget about the coat and go about your business. But the coat is always with you, keeping you warm. Whenever you like, you can have the thought, *Am I wearing my coat, and is it keeping me warm?* Immediately your awareness effortlessly shifts to your coat and you know it to be there. Then you become aware that the coat is keeping you warm. The coat is like pure awareness, and the warmth is Eufeeling.

Once your mind is accustomed to it, which could be almost immediately, it skips becoming aware of the coat and just becomes aware of the warmth—the reason you put the coat on in the first place.

Now let's say that you are used to living in the tropics but find yourself stranded in a secluded cabin in the deep north in winter. You come back from a walk and find that the lock to your cabin is frozen, and the key will not turn. This could be dangerous, and you immediately experience a flurry of anxious thoughts about your possible demise. Despite your envious tan, the thought of becoming a human Popsicle is not at all appealing. You become quite agitated and start running around pounding on doors and windows trying to get into the safety and warmth of your cabin. Then you remember that you are not wearing a Tommy Bahama pink-flamingo-patterned shirt but an arctic-proof coat to protect you against the cold. You realize that you are actually quite warm, and your mind begins to calm down. In that calmness you remember that you have a lighter in your coat pocket. You remove the lighter and heat your key and insert it into the lock. The warm key melts the ice and the lock turns, welcoming you into the warmth of your cabin.

Okay, I know this is an absurd analogy, but it will help to make my point about momentum. Becoming aware of your coat and the warmth it provided was calming for you. Your mind settled down and was able to think more clearly. Spontaneously you remembered the lighter in your coat pocket, and the solution to your problem was at hand.

If you do not do Quantum Entrainment and are not aware of Eufeeling, it is like living in the arctic in a short-sleeved flamingo shirt all the time. Because you are under-prepared, you are faced with one problem after another and live mostly in some state of agitation. You are completely at the mercy of the elements and sooner or later will end up looking like a flamingo-flavored Popsicle.

When you first start doing QE and becoming aware of Eufeeling, it is like you live in your flamingo shirt but put on your coat when you have a challenge confront you. You forget you have a coat until you have a problem. When you reach momentum, it is like you are always wearing your coat. You reap the benefits of continual protection, warmth, and well-being.

When you first learn QE, it is good to immediately begin the QE 90-Day Program to reach momentum. It is not like working out or going on a diet. The Becoming Fully Human Program is almost effortless and actually a lot of fun. In fact, you cannot force it or try to make it work. It only works if it is almost effortless. I say *almost* because in the beginning, you must become aware enough to become aware of Eufeeling, and this extra step requires some shift of attention from whatever you are doing to Eufeeling. But you will find it fascinating. And in a very short time (90 days or less), you will find you are living a vivid and prosperous existence.

The first step is this: multiply the number of years you have lived by four. If you have lived 45 years, then you would do 45 x 4 = 180. The number 180 represents the total of 90-day periods you have had in your life. Imagine how much fun and excitement you will have and what you will accomplish in the next 90-day period. Are you ready to start?

The QE 90-Day Program

- Play with QE continuously throughout the day. In the beginning you might want to place little sticky notes on your bathroom mirror, computer, car dashboard, refrigerator, and so on. What do you write on the notes? Nothing! It serves to remind you of pure awareness and what you have to do after you become aware of Eufeeling. As you make QE a "habit," you will be surprised how soon and effortlessly QE will manifest on its own.

- Do QE two to three times a day for at least ten minutes each. Many people do QE just after they wake up, before they go to sleep at night, and somewhere in the middle of their day to release stress and boost energy.

- Every day endeavor to do as many different kinds of QE as you can: Basic (touch) QE, Refined QE, QE Intention, Remote QE, Emotional QE, Self QE, Kid's QE, and Group/World Peace QE. Do QE with a pet, a stone, the sky, a candy bar . . .

- Do QE for others often. Give it away. You don't need their permission because you aren't doing anything. Just do it, lots of it.

- Don't look for results. Let them sneak up and surprise you. Just do QE, and go on with your normal affairs.

- Have fun and enjoy QE for what it is—a natural expression of harmonious living, of being fully human. And remember: *If it isn't easy and it isn't fun, then it isn't QE.*

CLOSING

Well my friends, it is time we bid adieu. (Does anybody talk like that anymore? Fun, isn't it?) I have really enjoyed our time together, and I am already looking forward to when we next meet. In the meantime, enjoy discovering your new world, the one seen through the eyes of Eufeeling. It really is a beautiful perspective on the mundane. That's right: your life will not appear different in the common ways, but it *will* be fundamentally different. You will come to know more of the sameness that unites the differences. You will find it friendly and familiar and yet altogether fresh.

This world, your world, is perfect just as it is. What you have begun will open you to that perfection. You will find it in the most remarkably ordinary places: the concentrated attention of a child learning to write, a blade of grass pushing through a crack in the sidewalk, a glint in the eye of an aged face. You will find it in your Self, waiting like a mother whose child has been too long away. This world comes out of Eufeeling. It is meant to be lived in and loved. At its depths, before it splinters into the infinite shards of the phenomenal worlds of mind and matter, it is still. You know that stillness. You have embraced it repeatedly during this time. It is yours. It is you. Do not waste this part of you. Be a friend to it, and visit it every day. Let it visit you in your world. Let it fill you with its presence and its peace. Let the worry and the whirl of the world touch you not, settled safely in the arms of silence. You, my friend, are a most precious reflection of that which shines in us all. Congratulations and welcome home.

THE STORY OF NOTHING, AND HOW IT IS CHANGING THE WORLD

As a boy, I lived in post–World War II Japan. I remember doing the things that all boys love: catching bees in a jar, making forts with rocks and sticks in the dirt, and lying on my back watching puffy white clouds slide across a deep cerulean sky. The child's eye is the saint's eye. But that all changes, doesn't it? It was at this time that I had my first spiritual awakening. I had become discouraged and angry with my practice of judo. I was sitting, frustrated and fuming on the tatami mat, when my sensei taught me a mind-over-matter technique that drained me of anger and filled me with inner quiet. I was surprised by joy.

All through my adolescence and young adulthood, I read about and practiced yoga, breathing techniques, and meditation. I was able to keep alive the child's eye even as I went to college, married, and started a family. In the early 1970s, I became a teacher of Transcendental Meditation and studied the Science of Creative Intelligence (SCI) under the gentle guidance of Maharishi Mahesh Yogi. Later, SCI became the foundation for deeper exploration into the realm beyond the mind—pure awareness.

For 15 years, I deeply dedicated myself to spiritual exploration. My daily routine included three and a half hours of meditation, with additional time devoted to studying and teaching spiritual practices. I accumulated nearly three years of silent, deep meditation literally sequestered on mountaintops in the French and Swiss Alps for months at a time. The driving force behind my dedication was that most exalted and utterly elusive state of enlightenment. I felt that I could become enlightened by strength of will and austere and obscure practices.

During this time, I had many deep and meaningful spiritual experiences. I began to resonate on finer and finer levels of existence. I spent time learning on the level of angels and sat in on the teachings of the ascended masters. I found the form of God and watched it dissolve into the formless essence of God-stuff. Ultimately, I became aware of pure awareness, the all-permeating Nothing from which all is born and into which all dissolves again.

I found myself with a foot in two worlds: the competitive world of day-to-day living and the ethereal realms of subtle beings and soft surrender. It was not an easy time for me physically or emotionally. It was difficult to remain focused on my family and profession when the serene silence of the "other" world lay beckoning from every shimmering form.

In the late 1980s, I met with a small group of spiritual seekers to study and practice meditative techniques. It was at that time that I started receiving instruction from my disincarnate teacher, the destroyer of ignorance, Siva. I passed the techniques along to the group, and we practiced them and passed them along to others. These techniques were the precursors to Quantum Entrainment. We could heal, give readings, and even encourage the experience of peace in others. I taught for seven years, but when I looked inwardly to see if I had moved any closer to enlightenment, I could not honestly say that I had. I looked at those following my teachings and found that they could inspire healing and interest in esoteric practices but they, too, failed to show me any significant inner growth. So in the mid-1990s, I walked away from my students and my teachings and began to look deeply inside for an answer to my lifelong quest for freedom from suffering.

I decided to remove anything from my life that did not encourage enlightenment and began removing everything that didn't work. It was a process that lasted seven more years. This time became the most painful of my life. During that period, I ended a 30-year marriage, gave up my teaching, dissolved my chiropractic practice, fell in and out of love, and moved away from friends and family to a city where I was virtually alone. It was then that I began writing *Beyond Happiness: Finding and Fulfilling Your Deepest Desire.*

I discovered during that time that nothing I had done was working. In my new home, alone and without direction, I became very ill. I laid in bed day after day under the dark cloud of depression while my body finally succumbed to the accumulated years of stress and disappointment. I developed physical maladies that drained me and made it impossible to think clearly. I couldn't write for ten months.

During the time of deepest darkness, I had a remarkable awakening unlike any I had experienced before. It stood out like a beacon in the blackness of night. In a single flash of insight, I cognized that nothing moves; that all created things and thoughts are nonmoving reflections of pure awareness. In fact, in some way I cannot explain, form does not exist. Form and movement are one and the same nonmoving emptiness. Any effort to explain this experience is laughably inadequate. Whether I can explain this cognition or not, it resonates deep within the stillness that is my essence (not my essence but *the* Essence). It is from here that I think and work and love and cry. It was at this time that the mechanics of creation began to open to my awareness. It is from here that QE was born, and I began to learn to heal.

It took some years more before the full impact of my cognition took hold. In fact, I am still watching the process unfold. It is as if the reflection of pure awareness I call "me" has to be infused with fullness slowly over apparent time. And so, without effort I have observed a quiet metamorphosis from the inside out. All the while I am both at peace and in apparent turmoil. My life is as it was before. I get frustrated, angry, sad, and happy. I become temporarily overshadowed by the human condition but return quickly and without effort renewed to inner quiet like a pristine meadow after a summer thundershower. But my life—or, more accurately, this life—is also unfathomable, free from form and function, free to be . . . nothing.

I kept saying to myself that nothing works. Then I realized that nothing did work. That is, the "nothing" of pure awareness is the only thing that works, and that's because it is nothing. All the time I was meditating and reading and teaching, I had a goal to be free of suffering. As long as I had a goal, then I wasn't satisfied where I was. You see? A goal creates a path, and a path takes you away from where you are. But my cognition showed that the nothing of pure awareness is everywhere, all the time. In other words, there is nowhere to go and nothing you can do to get peace because it is already where you are. You can't get something you already have. All you need to do is become aware that you have it, right? A goal and a path are illusions. They take the mind away from nonmoving awareness and involve it in the illusory world of good and bad, right and wrong, fleeting happiness and ultimate suffering.

So herein lies the core of my teaching: *You do not need to do anything to be aware of pure awareness. You already have pure awareness, so you only need to become aware of it.* All the time I spent in deep meditation and studying to become free of suffering only deepened my suffering. It wasn't necessary. Only awareness of pure awareness is needed to be free, and that is the simplest thing in existence.

Not quite two years ago, I was quietly contemplating the plight of humanity on Earth. I wondered how our suffering might be replaced with the inner peace that has been extolled throughout the ages by saints and sages alike. I wondered why so many of us turn outward—away from inner bliss—to embrace the fleeting pleasures of the senses. It was that simple inquiry that opened my consciousness to the genius of what I would later call QE. Please know that I take no credit for this insight. I don't even take authorship for asking the question. In reality, both the question and the answer are superfluous, but that's a story for another time.

What I realized was that our wayward minds have to somehow be excited about something before they will pay proper attention. So I offered the mind the thought of instant healing. That got it interested initially, but the problem is that the nothing of pure awareness isn't exciting to our minds. Actually, our senses can never experience pure awareness, and our minds will never understand it. So what can we do? My challenge was to interest the mind in something that could not be experienced and teach it something that could not be understood. Then the mind had to remain in this non-experience state of pure awareness long enough to feel the harmonious effects on body and mind. This would have to be a very fast process, for the mind is extremely restless. The answer was given in the form of the Eufeeling, a stroke of utter genius. The Eufeeling balances the mind between the absolute nonmovement of pure awareness and its impulsive, constant activity. The Eufeeling holds the mind there until not only the initiator's body-mind benefits but also the partner he or she is working with. It was a most remarkable and completely unique idea. I couldn't wait to try it out.

When I did try it out, I was overwhelmed by the speed and depth of healing of this new process. Next I tried to teach it and found that others could learn the QE process as quickly and easily as the process was practiced. Several months after discovering QE, I wrote *The Secret of Instant Healing* so that people around the world could learn how to experience pure awareness through healing.

⊙

As I write this, the German translation of *The Secret of Instant Healing (Quantenheilung)* has been the number one–selling book in both the Natural Healing and Esoteric categories for the last two years. This was achieved by word of mouth, and the word continues to spread. The rest of Europe—indeed, the rest of the world from Australia to Austria and Angola to Estonia—is beginning to awaken to the joyful potential of QE.

All in all, the growth of QE has been phenomenal when you consider it was born just six years ago and is still in its infancy. Then again, it shouldn't be surprising because one of the first intentions I cradled in my mind after developing QE was for the rapid spread of QE and, with it, harmony in this world. It seems that the future of QE is tied to the future fortune of our world. The particulars of world peace, ecological instability, poverty, and the like have no simple solution, at least not by working on the same level of disharmony that created them. Discordant thinking must necessarily reflect discordant action. The answer to world harmony is not in the particulars but in the realization of our very inner, harmonious nature. Just as the insidious nature of chaotic thinking has weakened our world, so, too, the nurturing rays of Self can heal it. I believe that QE will add the necessary spiritual leverage to create the tipping point for peace. Then we will achieve, as a whole, what only a few isolated luminaries have so far realized. We will be at rest, complete, reflecting perfect harmony in a world at peace with its Self.

GLOSSARY

Common Consciousness: Consciousness *unaware* of Self, of Eufeeling. Common consciousness is subservient to the fear and prejudice of ego; generally destructive even when intentions are positive. One feels that they are the initiator of their actions; that they are the creator of things and thoughts. The prevalent form of consciousness in the world. The opposite of *QE Awareness.*

Ego: The loss of awareness of Eufeeling resulting in the illusion of individuality. It is the controlling entity of the unaware mind. Ego is born of fear, which is both its foil and its fuel. It wants to be whole and merge with Eufeeling but fears assimilation by it. Ego tries to eliminate what it cannot control. It feels that if it can control everything, it can be whole. It is the primal cause of suffering. Time, fear, and ego are one and the same. Ego is an illusion. QE Awareness eliminates ego's destructive influence over the mind not by destroying it but expanding it to infinity.

Eufeeling: Eufeeling ("euphoric feeling") is a perception of wholeness, of the first glimmering of awareness in the mind. The natural state of human awareness. Eufeeling is timeless and cannot die. The mind recognizes Eufeeling as pure peace, stillness, joy, compassion, love, bliss, and so forth. The lens through which pure awareness creates. The foundation for QE Awareness. Eufeeling and *Self* are synonymous.

Mistake of the Ego: The false idea that ego can fill the void left by separation from Eufeeling by filling its existence with material things, mental concepts, and the play of emotions. Movement of the mind outward away from Eufeeling.

Pure Awareness: Awareness of that which is unchanging, without beginning or end. Awareness of Nothing. The state of no thoughts, the gap. One is not aware of pure awareness while it is happening. Beyond energy and form. Every created thing is the unmoving, nonexistent illusion of pure awareness.

Pure Eufeeling: The perception of Eufeeling before it takes form in the mind. The experience of awareness of pure awareness while remaining aware; not thought, not feeling, but still aware. The state from which miracles are created. Spontaneous materialization of corporeal form like the fishes and the loaves, sacred ash, instantaneous healing of disease. The purest state of individual awareness.

Quantum Entrainment (QE): The effortless process of guiding common consciousness to pure awareness and then remaining aware of Eufeeling. QE is successful when it stops working in pure awareness.

QE Awareness: Action performed while aware of Eufeeling. Awareness beyond the bonds of cause and effect, free of fear and disharmony. One becomes the observer as creation takes place through them, not from them. The opposite of *Common Consciousness.*

QE Intention: The effortless fulfillment of desire while aware of Eufeeling. Immediately resolves emotional disharmony and attachment to desire while organizing the forces of creation around satisfying the desire on the material plane. Fulfillment of the primal, deepest desire to be reunited with inner Self, free of fear. Desiring without ego. Always gives more than is asked for. Creates from perfect harmony. Cannot oppose the basic creative forces. Can do no harm.

Self: See *Eufeeling.*

Self-Awareness: See *QE Awareness.*

ABOUT THE AUTHOR

Dr Frank J. Kinslow has been researching and teaching healing techniques for more than 35 years. He draws from his clinical experience as a chiropractic physician, in-depth studies into Eastern esoteric philosophies and practices, and an ardent love of relativity and quantum physics. In 2007, the Quantum Entrainment process of instant healing was born out of a personal crisis that left Dr Kinslow with *nowhere to go and nothing to do.* Out of this *nothing,* he was able to create a vibrant and fulfilling life for himself. He began to teach and write with such simplicity and clarity that in just a few years, tens of thousands of people around the world were able to create vibrant and fulfilling lives for themselves just by reading his books.

Dr Kinslow is a chiropractic physician, a teacher for the deaf and a Doctor of Clinical Spiritual Counseling. He continues to write and teach extensively. He resides in Sarasota, Florida, with his wife, Martina.

www.kinslowsystem.com

ABOUT THE KINSLOW SYSTEM ORGANIZATION

Dr. Kinslow is the originator of The Kinslow System and sole teacher of Quantum Entrainment. He conducts seminars and lectures worldwide. For more information about The Kinslow System and Quantum Entrainment, please contact us at:

Website: **www.KinslowSystem.com**
E-mail: **Info@KinslowSystem.com**
Phone: **(877) 811-5287** (toll-free in North America)

Kinslow System Products

Books

The Secret of Instant Healing

The Secret of Quantum Living

The Secret of Everyday Bliss

Beyond Happiness: Finding and Fulfilling Your Deepest Desire

Martina and the Ogre (a QE children's book)

Audio Books

The Secret of Instant Healing

The Secret of Quantum Living

Eufeeling! The Art of Creating Inner Peace and Outer Prosperity

Beyond Happiness: Finding and Fulfilling Your Deepest Desire

CDs

Exercises for Quantum Living (2-CD set)

Exercises for Quantum Living for Two (2-CD set)

Quantum Entrainment Exercises

Martina and the Ogre (a QE children's book)

DVDs

Quantum Entrainment Introductory Presentation

What the Bleep QE Video

Martina and the Ogre (a QE children's book) (Blu-ray DVD)

Other services found at **www.KinslowSystem.com**:

- The Kinslow System Blog
- Social Networks
- The QE Quill [Free] Newsletter
- Free Downloads
- The QE Forum
- The Kinslow System Videos & Pictures

Hay House Titles of Related Interest

YOU CAN HEAL YOUR LIFE, the movie,
starring Louise L. Hay & Friends
(available as a 1-DVD programme and an expanded 2-DVD set)
Watch the trailer at: **www.LouiseHayMovie.com**

THE SHIFT, the movie,
starring Dr Wayne W. Dyer
(available as a 1-DVD programme and an expanded 2-DVD set)
Watch the trailer at: **www.DyerMovie.com**

⊙

INSIDE-OUT HEALING: Transforming Your Life
Through the Power of Presence, by Richard Moss

THE MINDFUL MANIFESTO: How Doing Less and Noticing
More Can Help Us Thrive in a Stressed-out World, by Dr Jonty
Heaversedge & Ed Halliwell

THE POWER OF SELF-HEALING: Unlock Your Natural Healing
Potential in 21 Days!, by Dr Fabrizio Mancini

RESONANCE: Nine Practices for Harmonious Health and Vitality,
by Joyce Hawkes, PhD

TRANSCENDENTAL MEDITATION: The Classic Text Revised
and Updated, by Jack Forem

WISHES FULFILLED: Mastering the Art of Manifesting,
by Dr Wayne W. Dyer

All of the above are available at your local bookstore,
or may be ordered by contacting Hay House (see next page).

⊙

We hope you enjoyed this Hay House book. If you'd like to receive our online catalogue featuring additional information on Hay House books and products, or if you'd like to find out more about the Hay Foundation, please contact:

Hay House UK, Ltd.,
Astley House, 33 Notting Hill Gate, London W11 3JQ
Phone: 0-20-3675-2450 • *Fax:* 0-20-3675-2451
www.hayhouse.co.uk • **www.hayfoundation.org**

Published and distributed in the United States by:
Hay House, Inc., P.O. Box 5100, Carlsbad, CA 92018-5100
Phone: (760) 431-7695 or (800) 654-5126
Fax: (760) 431-6948 or (800) 650-5115
www.hayhouse.com®

Published and distributed in Australia by: Hay House Australia Pty.
Ltd., 18/36 Ralph St., Alexandria NSW 2015 • *Phone:* 612-9669-4299
Fax: 612-9669-4144 • www.hayhouse.com.au

Published and distributed in the Republic of South Africa by:
Hay House SA (Pty), Ltd., P.O. Box 990, Witkoppen 2068
Phone/Fax: 27-11-467-8904 • www.hayhouse.co.za

Published in India by: Hay House Publishers India, Muskaan
Complex, Plot No. 3, B-2, Vasant Kunj, New Delhi 110 070
Phone: 91-11-4176-1620 • *Fax:* 91-11-4176-1630
www.hayhouse.co.in

Distributed in Canada by: Raincoast,
9050 Shaughnessy St., Vancouver, B.C. V6P 6E5 •
Phone: (604) 323-7100 • *Fax:* (604) 323-2600 • www.raincoast.com

⊙

Take Your Soul on a Vacation

Visit **www.HealYourLife.com**® to regroup,
recharge, and reconnect with your own magnificence.
Featuring blogs, mind-body-spirit news, and
life-changing wisdom from Louise Hay and friends.

Visit **www.HealYourLife.com** today!

JOIN THE HAY HOUSE FAMILY

As the leading self-help, mind, body and spirit publisher in the UK, we'd like to welcome you to our family so that you can enjoy all the benefits our website has to offer.

 EXTRACTS from a selection of your favourite author titles

 COMPETITIONS, PRIZES & SPECIAL OFFERS Win extracts, money off, downloads and so much more

 LISTEN to a range of radio interviews and our latest audio publications

 CELEBRATE YOUR BIRTHDAY An inspiring gift will be sent your way

 **LATEST NEWS** Keep up with the latest news from and about our authors

 ATTEND OUR AUTHOR EVENTS Be the first to hear about our author events

 **iPHONE APPS** Download your favourite app for your iPhone

 HAY HOUSE INFORMATION Ask us anything, all enquiries answered

join us online at **www.hayhouse.co.uk**

 Astley House, 33 Notting Hill Gate, London W11 3JQ
T: 020 3675 2450 E: info@hayhouse.co.uk